THE REMINISCENCES OF
Rear Admiral Edmond J. Moran
U.S. Naval Reserve (Retired)

INTERVIEWED BY
Dr. John T. Mason, Jr.

U.S. Naval Institute • Annapolis, Maryland

Copyright © 2004

Preface

The name Moran has been synonymous with maritime towing for more than a century. An individual who spanned a great deal of that time in the course of his professional career was the late Rear Admiral Edmond J. Moran, who served for many years as head of the Moran Towing Corporation. It has been a family-run business since the 19th century and remains so today.

This oral history is an unusual one in the Naval Institute collection in that it contains the recollections of an individual who was not a career naval officer. He did, however, intersect with the Navy on a number of occasions, most notably during the 20th century's two great World Wars. In the first, he was an enlisted man and junior officer who was involved with commercial ships taken over by the Navy to serve in the Naval Overseas Transport Service. He made several voyages to Europe during that war.

His most notable naval duty was in World War II, during which he played several roles. He left the presidency of his company to serve with the government for the duration of the conflict. During part of that time he served with the U.S. Maritime Commission in taking over civilian craft for government service. Then he became much more active with the Navy. He served on the staff of Commander Eastern Sea Frontier in monitoring shipping in the Atlantic and coordinating rescue operations when necessary. Later he made a key contribution to one of the great amphibious operations of the war, the Allied invasion of Normandy, France, in June 1944. Because the invading soldiers were landing over open beaches, rather than harbors, the ships that brought the soldiers' supplies and equipment needed protection from the waves and swells of the English Channel in order to unload. The answer came in the form of artificial harbors, and that meant towing the components of those harbors from England. And that called for an individual with a great deal of tugboat expertise. Moran supervised the successful operation of towing the breakwaters into place and was lauded for his work by the top Allied military and naval leaders.

The oral history covers several other topics as well, including Admiral Moran's charming descriptions of learning tugboat operations when he was a youngster. His mentor was a wise and caring stepfather who worked for the Moran Company. Captain Willard Searle, at one time the Navy's Supervisor of Salvage, joined the oral history's principal interviewer, Dr. John Mason, to facilitate Admiral Moran's discussion of the role of tugboats in rescue and salvage operations. Still another facet of the memoir is the insight it provides into Moran's character and personality—his sense of integrity, his leadership qualities, friendliness, and the energetic approach that enabled him to move ahead in both his naval and civilian careers.

I have incorporated into the transcript a number of changes provided by Admiral Moran and have done a bit of light editing. Even so, this transcript is quite similar to the version in the oral interviews. In addition, I have inserted footnotes to provide further information for readers who use the volume.

Finally, the Naval Institute expresses its gratitude to the Tawani Foundations and the Pritzker Military Library for their generous financial support of the oral history program that produced this memoir.

Paul Stillwell
Director, History Division
U.S. Naval Institute
March 2004

ADMIRAL EDMOND J. MORAN

REAR ADMIRAL
EDMOND J. MORAN, USNR
(ret.)

Admiral Edmond J. Moran, born in Brooklyn on October 13, 1896, died at his home in New Canaan, Ct., on July 15, 1993. He had joined the family business in 1915, starting as a clerk after graduation from school. The firm had been founded by his grandfather Michael, an Irish immigrant, in 1860. Over the years, Edmond Moran would work in every part of the shore-side operations before becoming chairman of the board of directors in 1964. Even before he came into the office, however, he was no stranger to the industry, having spent his vacations from school working aboard the company tugs. This familiarity with life and conditions aboard the tugs would prove invaluable in World War II years when he directed the crews of the multinational fleet of 160 tugs and barges.

World War I had interrupted Admiral Moran's career and he joined the U.S. Naval Reserve in 1917, receiving a commission as an Ensign. He served at sea as a watch officer on supply ships and was released from active duty as a Lieutenant (j.g.) in 1919. He returned to the company and went on to be elected president of Moran Towing and Transportation Company in April 8th, 1941.

In the spring of 1941, when the war in Europe was escalating, Admiral Moran was called to Washington to act as a consultant to the U.S. Maritime Commission. This federal agency was responsible for building, operating and training crews for the expanding war-time fleet of the merchant marine. The United States, even before entering the war, had a commitment to the British government to supply a fleet of tugs under the lend-lease program. Admiral Moran used his extensive knowledge of the tug and barge industry to negotiate for the sale of vessels and deliver them to England.

When the United States entered the war after Pearl Harbor in 1941, the Admiral resigned his position as president of the company for the duration, and activated his commission in the U.S. Naval Reserve. He went to Washington as a Lieutenant Commander and became director of small boat procurement for the War Shipping Administration, a branch of the U.S. Maritime Commission. It was his duty to assemble a fleet of some 2,000 vessels from the civilian sector for the war effort and determine that owners would receive just compensation from the government for their vessels.

A short time after the United States entered the war, in January of 1942, the German Navy launched operation "Drum Roll," a concentration of their submarine fleet on the East Coast of the United States. Submarine captains found easy targets of merchant ships sailing alone, without any armed escorts, outlined from the lights of the coastal cities. Allied ships, mostly tankers, were sunk within sight of land, right outside the major east coast ports, including New York. The then LCDR Moran was "borrowed" from the Maritime Commission and assigned as rescue officer, under the commander of the Eastern Sea Frontier. His job was to dispatch rescue tugs to the aid of torpedoed ships and crews. At a time when the nation had an acute shortage of ships, his efforts enabled many damaged vessels to be repaired and returned to sea again.

When the Battle of the Atlantic turned in the Allies favor, with the introduction of the convoy system including Naval escorts and air support, the Admiral returned to the WSA. In addition to his duties in vessel procurement, he became director of the tug and barge department. Included in this program was the construction of the famous wartime fleet of V-4 tugs. These 195-foot long deep-sea tugs, with 2,500 h.p.

WEDNESDAY, JUNE 7, 1944
The Phoenix, concrete caissons have been towed across the English channel on D-day, plus one, by the seagoing tugs. In the painting by Dwight Shepler, the smaller harbor tugs take over, maneuvering the caissons in place in the shallow waters off the French beach before they were filled with sea water, sinking to become the man-made harbor for the Mulberry, Normandy beachhead. Admiral Moran was in complete charge of all the tugs and barges in the invasion.

diesel engines, many operated by Moran with civilian merchant marine crews, played a major role in the war at sea.

The Germans knew that the invasion of Europe would be impossible for the Allies without a major port to land supplies and therefore concentrated their defense against the invasion on the French channel ports of Cherbourg and LeHavre. It was estimated that it would take six tons of supplies for every soldier landed on the beach. The planners of the Normandy invasion, however, included the innovation of man-made ports, code named "Mulberry" and "Gooseberry."

Admiral Harold R. Stark USN, commander of U.S. Navy forces in Europe, came to Washington with some questions on towing problems for the upcoming invasion and consulted Edmond Moran. Later the Army brought up the problem of landing 1,000 tons of supplies directly on the beaches with a five-foot draft barge. Admiral Moran knew just the equipment and where to find it. He suggested the New York Harbor railroad car floats and shallow draft gasoline barges. These crafts, never meant to venture outside of the placid waters of the harbor, were sent in a convoy with some small tugs, across the Atlantic to England for the invasion.

The then Commodore Moran, was asked by Stark to go to England and look at the proposed towing plans. He was first assigned to planning the artificial harbors as an advisor but was quickly recognized as and expert in tugs and towing. In answer to an interviewers questions some years later, Admiral Moran said " I was given complete charge of the whole operation, command of all the tugs, barges and floats, everything connected with the towing phase of the operation." He set up a base in Les-on-Solent, England and took charge over more senior officers. His tact and experience in dealing with the multi-national captains and crews, many of whom were civilian tugboat men, including those working for Moran, proved invaluable. The tugs towed the man-made harbors to the beachheads, reaching France on June 7th, just one day after the invasion, and supplies started to flow to the landing troops.

Historians now agree, with the military leaders of the time, that the success of the D-day invasion on June 6th, 1944 and the liberation of western Europe would not have been possible without the man-made harbors. For his part in D-day, Admiral Edmond J. Moran was awarded the Legion of Merit by the United States, Honorary Commander, Military Division, Order of the British Empire; and the Croix de Guerre, with gold stars from the French Government.

The Admiral went on to Guam in the Pacific to repeat the preparations for a similar man-made harbors to be used in the proposed invasion of Japan when the war ended. In August of 1953, Edmond J. Moran was promoted to Rear Admiral, United States Naval Reserve. Admiral Moran returned to the family business in 1946 and was elected chairman of the board of directors in February of 1964. His leadership of the company during the expanding postwar years has been credited with helping make Moran one of the largest and most successful in the marine towing industry worldwide. He retired after serving 69 years with the company in 1984, turning over the chairmanship to his oldest son, Thomas E. Moran, present chairman of the board of directors of the Moran Corporation and a fourth generation of the founding family.

Admiral Moran was an active member and leader in the American Maritime Industry. He served three terms as president of the Maritime Association of the Port of New York & New Jersey. He was on the Board of Managers of the American Bureau of Shipping. The Admiral served as a member of the Board of Directors of the South Street Seaport Museum, New York City, Chubb Insurance Company, Victory Carriers, Propeller Club of New York and as a trustee of the Museum of the City of New York. He served as president of the India House and was a member of the New York Yacht Club, both in New York City. He was vice-chairman of Fordham University's trustees and was awarded an honorary doctorate of letters degree from that University. Admiral Moran was given Papal Honors in 1980.

Admiral Moran is survived by three sons, Thomas E. of Darien, Connecticut, Kevin P. of New York City and Edmond J. of Baltimore, Maryland and three daughters, Nancy Grinder of Aiken, S.C., Margot Danis of St. Louis, Mo., Sheila Reynolds of New York City. Survivors included 14 grandchildren and 18 great grandchildren. He was married for 63 years to the former Alice Laux, who died several years ago.

Authorization

The U.S. Naval Institute is hereby authorized to make available to individuals, libraries, and other repositories of its choosing the transcripts of five oral history interviews concerning the life and career of the late Rear Admiral Edmond J. Moran, U.S. Naval Reserve (Retired). The interviews were recorded on 20 May 1977, 8 June 1977, 7 October 1977, 17 October 1977, and 21 September 1978, in collaboration with Dr. John T. Mason, Jr., for the U.S. Naval Institute.

The undersigned does hereby release and assign to the U.S. Naval Institute all right, title, restrictions, and interest in the interviews. The copyright in both the oral and transcribed versions shall be the sole property of the U.S. Naval Institute. The tape recordings of the interviews are and will remain the property of the U.S. Naval Institute.

Signed and sealed this _____ day of _____ 1994.

_____
Thomas E. Moran, for the estate of
Rear Admiral Edmond J. Moran, USNR (Ret.)

Interview Number 1 with Rear Admiral Edmond J. Moran, U.S. Naval Reserve (Retired)
Place: Admiral Moran's office in the World Trade Center, New York City
Date: Friday, 20 May 1977
Interviewer: John T. Mason, Jr.

John T. Mason, Jr.: I have been looking forward to this series of interviews with you. Your career has certainly been a most interesting one in a most interesting field. I am happy to know that we are going to have a permanent record of your activities. Would you begin this spoken biography in the proper way by giving me the date and place of your birth?

Admiral Moran: I was born in Brooklyn, New York, in the autumn of 1896 and educated in public and private schools there until the summer of 1915, when I joined the Moran Towing business in New York City, organized in 1860 by my grandfather, who died in 1906, and where I have remained except for two periods of U.S. naval service.

John T. Mason, Jr.: Would you, at this point, tell me something about your grandfather. You knew him, not very well because you were so young.

Admiral Moran: My grandfather was born in Ireland in 1832.[*] He came here at the age of 18 and went to the Erie Canal, which was then called, prospectively, "Clinton's Folly," and there he worked as a youngster driving mules and such work as one of the age of 18 could competently undertake. A few years after, he accumulated sufficient funds to look forward to a career in business. He came to New York, where he found that he could invest about $2,500 as half of an interest in a tugboat. He found the vessel, he did so, and that was the commencement in 1860 of his business career.

John T. Mason, Jr.: He must have been a very ambitious young lad.

---

[*] Michael Moran (1832-1906).

Admiral Moran: He was; he was a tireless worker; he was a gracious kind of man; he was charitable; he was compassionate; and no effort was ever spared, that I could discover, to help anyone who needed whatever he had.

My father died in 1902 and left my mother with my sister and me to care for and to educate.

John T. Mason, Jr.: Was his death a sudden thing?

Admiral Moran: My grandfather's death was, to a degree, sudden. He was over 72 years of age, and in those days life didn't have a much longer expectancy.

John T. Mason, Jr.: But your father was a relatively young man.

Admiral Moran: My father was a young man; he died at the age of 37. During 1905 my mother married Thomas Reynolds, a seagoing tug master who was employed by the company, then known as the Moran Towing Company, which was being operated by two of my uncles—my father's brothers.* My stepfather took an active interest in my general well-being and frequently had me with him on coastwise and ocean voyages. I spent summer vacations, every available holiday, and one time a longer period while my sister's illness quarantined our home and I was not able to stay there.

John T. Mason, Jr.: You must have liked doing this, did you?

Admiral Moran: I enjoyed it.

John T. Mason, Jr.: Had you determined at that early age to be a part of the family business?

Admiral Moran: I hadn't really, but what I learned with my stepfather as a boy came to me with no effort at all on my part, because it required nothing more than watching with

---

* Eugene F. Moran and Joseph Moran.

interest where we were going, what we were doing, and what everyone else was doing on the tug. These occasions were, in a sense, in the nature of holidays. I learned, without being aware of it, the business of going to sea. After a few short years and at an early age, I knew the compass, could read charts, steer a course, knew basic rules to prevent collisions, could fix a position, knew chipping, painting, and simple maintenance work.

I could not, naturally, deal with the heavy or arduous tasks of a seaman, but I knew when and how their duties should be done. I was small in stature, so my stepfather felt I would never be an able seaman, but he felt that I could eventually handle a mate's berth and ultimately, a master's. It would, of course, be difficult for me to qualify for a license as a master or pilot without active performance and gainful employment, but there was hope that the then Steamboat Inspection Service would accept a certification by three competent sources when I would be able to be ready for an examination.

John T. Mason, Jr.: Mr. Reynolds must have been a remarkable kind of teacher to have taught you all these things without your realizing that he was teaching you.

Admiral Moran: That's right. I used to go with him, and then on my first trip I ever made, went with him to Philadelphia—outside, down the coast, and up the Delaware Bay. When we got offshore, it was kind of rough, so he put me to bed in a little settee that he had in his own room, and I didn't wake up until the next day when we were going up the Delaware. He watched out for me. He was an uneducated man from a scholastic point of view, and he had trouble spelling.

John T. Mason, Jr.: As so many people did in that generation.

Admiral Moran: Oh, sure. We would go places, and he would say to me, "How do you spell 'transportation'?" which he knew. He could see it on the electrical signs in the river—the transportation companies—and he would ask me to spell "transportation" or spell "company." He knew French and English words, and he would ask me to spell those words for him. Then he would ask me to write too. He wrote; it wasn't too legible, but it wasn't—

John T. Mason, Jr.: Very sparse.

Admiral Moran: Yes. He was very competent in his job, and he would teach me. When he would blow a whistle signal—one whistle to alter my course to starboard; two whistles, I would alter my course to port; three whistles, my engines are going astern. And when he would blow those whistles, or order those whistles to be blown, he would say, "What am I going to do now, or what are we going to do now?" Or when he would send a signal to the engine room, he would say, "What will we do now?"—whether we were going astern or going ahead at full speed, or half speed, or slowing down, or stopped. I learned the signals that we would send to the engine room, and I would plan the reaction to the signals. It took no skill whatever, just to be able to remember.

John T. Mason, Jr.: Perfectly natural.

Admiral Moran: Just the most natural thing. And then he would have signals for working capstans and winches. At nighttime, after dark, passing vessels, he would ask me, "What's that green light?" or "What's that red light?" "What are those two lights up there, or three lights, or one light, or the light on the masthead and the light on the mainmast?" He would tell me how much power we were exerting in terms of horsepower, and then he would tell me about another vessel. He would say, "That vessel has 400 horsepower." Then at nighttime, he would say, "That's the *Atlantic*," or "That's the *Brooklyn*," a tug passing. The arrangements of the lights were all he had to identify the equipment, because the lights were situated on every vessel in a different kind of way. When you were accustomed to it, you would know the vessels from the lights.

He would tell me about the ferryboats; he would tell the route of the ferryboat just from the location of the running lights. He would show me charts when he would lay out a course: "This is where we are, and this is where we're going, and this is the way we go. And the reason I know this is the way we go is that I take the line from this position to the one we are going to and apply it to a compass rose, on the course, and that's the way we do it."

John T. Mason, Jr.: This is essential in navigation?

Admiral Moran: This was to fix courses and things like that.

John T. Mason, Jr.: What about the stars?

Admiral Moran: I never touched that. And he didn't do much about stars either. He wasn't a great celestial navigator. He was more a coastwise pilot, and he knew a great many courses that he had in his little book that he used to keep in his pocket for ready reference in case he felt he wasn't certain or that the course we were looking at on the compass didn't appear to be the one he used to go on. Another route might have been more acceptable.

John T. Mason, Jr.: There was so much shipping in New York Harbor at that time; how was it policed? How was it controlled?

Admiral Moran: There were no controls on it; it was just the skill of the man in the harbor who knew where the other fellow was going and kept out of his way as a matter of courtesy. And there was a good deal of the kind of thing that you see the courteous automobile driver confer to another person on the road.

John T. Mason, Jr.: You don't see much of that now, but this was true on the water?

Admiral Moran: It was true on the water; you had great respect for the other fellow, the size of his tow. The weight of his burden really would always be a concession to someone who was willing to take a little time and let another fellow pass. Or a big ship that needed all the water that was in the channel, that couldn't vary its course much, would always be given right of way over someone who would have the right of way but didn't need the depth that the ship needed. That kind of thing prevailed in those days. I think it may still, for all I know, because I don't go out there.

Admiral Moran: The whole picture was complicated by the ferries plying back and forth all the time.

Admiral Moran: There were probably not less than eight or nine ferry routes in the North River, and in the East River from Brooklyn to Manhattan there were six or seven ferries crossing all the time.* Then there were, and still are, ferries running from the Battery to Staten Island.† Consideration has to be given to those vessels loaded with people—commuters.

John T. Mason, Jr.: Were there many collisions?

Admiral Moran: Not too many, considering the number of vessels in the harbor. I suppose that at the time I am talking about now, there were probably 450 tugs in operation all the time, 24 hours a day. There were probably as many as 2,000 barges and lighters and scows that carried equipment, case goods, grain, coal, petroleum products across the harbor, up and down, north and south on the Hudson River. Canal barges coming in with cargo loaded in the Great Lakes came down here for transshipment, coal from the Pennsylvania fields, and some Virginia coal came in here for powerhouses and domestic consumption. It was a very industrial port, a very, very busy place.

John T. Mason, Jr.: And, of course, all the transatlantic liners.

Admiral Moran: Transatlantic and coastwise liners carrying passengers and cargoes.

John T. Mason, Jr.: What provisions were made, or were there any regulations governing safety for the passenger liners?

---

* North River was a term used in years past for the lower part of the Hudson River, to the west of Manhattan.
† The Battery is at the lower tip of Manhattan Island.

Admiral Moran: The safety for the passengers was a provision inherent in the ship itself. The ships rarely had difficulty going or coming through the port. I don't remember any of the big passenger ships ever having a collision that involved the loss of life. There were excursion boats that carried people for short trips up the Hudson River or Long Island Sound on weekends or Saturdays, or sightseeing trips. In those cases there were at times collisions. At one time there was a very serious fire in an excursion vessel called the *General Slocum*.[*] The ship took fire, and I think there were 1,200 people lost. It was a very serious thing and caused great concern and caused, to a degree, a change in the rules for hoses and firefighting equipment.

John T. Mason, Jr.: And this was governed largely by the city of New York, I take it.

Admiral Moran: No, the operation of all vessels over, I think, 65 feet was under the jurisdiction of the Department of Commerce and implemented by the rules and regulations of the United States Steamboat Inspection Service.[†] It had the duty of inspecting the vessel for its suitability for the trade it was to be engaged in and also for the licensing of the personnel that would operate the ship, or vessel, or tug, or whatever it might have been.

John T. Mason, Jr.: Now, in the case of the Moran tugs, were you under contract to a line like the Cunard Line?

Admiral Moran: Yes. In earlier days a company wasn't as busy in the business of handling ships—docking and undocking and towing them in and about the harbor—as it became about 1917. It took more interest in that activity of the business and continued to do so until today.

---

[*] On 15 June 1904 the paddleboat *General Slocum* left New York City on a Sunday outing up the East River. On board were 1,358 passengers, most of whom were children. The steamboat was swept by a fire that could not be controlled. In all, at least 1,021 people were killed, and the death toll may have been higher.

[†] In 1942 the inspection duties once performed by the Steamboat Inspection Service were transferred to the Coast Guard. At the time the change was considered temporary, but it became permanent in 1946.

John T. Mason, Jr.: That is a very interesting picture you have given me, sir. Now you were about to be licensed.

Admiral Moran: My schooling was finished in the summer of 1915 when I took the position as office boy with the family company.

John T. Mason, Jr.: Tell me what kind of education you had. You said largely in the public and private schools, and also in your biography it says something about the Polytechnic Institute and the country day school.

Admiral Moran: No, it wasn't country day school; it was before that. It was the preparatory school for the Polytechnic Institute, which is a technical school, an engineering school—every aspect of engineering. I took the preparatory course and was finished with it in 1915. I was then 18 years old and would be 19 years old in October. I came to the company in the summer.

John T. Mason, Jr.: Was Mr. Reynolds prominent in the company then?

Admiral Moran: Yes, he was. He was in the company when my mother married him.

In 1915 I took a position as office boy in the family company in Manhattan. I received $5.00 a week as compensation and worked diligently for it. It was a ten-hour day, six days a week.

John T. Mason, Jr.: Tell me something about your duties as office boy. What did you have to do?

Admiral Moran: It was close to the life of the men, and at 18 years of age I was having something to do with that. My duties consisted of running errands, answering telephones, opening windows, closing them, cleaning them.

John T. Mason, Jr.: Opening the mail?

Admiral Moran: No, I wasn't trusted with the mail at that early date. I was engaged in mailing the outward stuff and carrying messages. The telephones were frequently used, but word-of-mouth messages and written messages were delivered to the tugs for fear of misunderstanding by the use of the telephone.

John T. Mason, Jr.: There was not a complete trust of the telephone?

Admiral Moran: No, not with what was regarded then as misunderstandings. I did the work of the office boy, answered messages, looked after the welfare of my uncles by bringing them lunch when they wanted it, doing everything that was needed. I used to go to the U.S. Engineer Office every day for permits to do certain kinds of work relating to the improvement of waterways. I was very busy.

John T. Mason, Jr.: How big was the office?

Admiral Moran: The office then consisted of a dispatcher, two accountants, a clerk, a stenographer, and a superintendent whose duty was to deal with maintenance and breakdown problems. That was the extent of it, in addition to my uncles.

John T. Mason, Jr.: Where were you located?

Admiral Moran: We were located on the fourth floor of the Whitehall Building. It's down there right at the Battery.

John T. Mason, Jr.: How many tugs did you have at that time approximately?

Admiral Moran: I think six tugs and about 20 scows. Scows are uncovered barges or lighters without any propulsion of their own or ability to do anything but just to take a load and bring it someplace. Someone would take the load off, or someone would put the load on—no capacity to load or discharge cargo.

John T. Mason, Jr.: A tugboat at that time would have a complement of how many men?

Admiral Moran: Probably, on a 24-hour basis, a captain and a mate, an engineer and an assistant, three deck hands, and a cook—seven or eight men—and they would go almost anywhere with that capacity of personnel.

I was also given the opportunity to expand my knowledge of the simple side and problems of business in the operation of the tugs.

John T. Mason, Jr.: This was in addition to what you learned as an office boy?

Admiral Moran: Yes.

John T. Mason, Jr.: Who was your tutor in this?

Admiral Moran: That was something, as someone would say, "Keep a record of the location of the scows and whom they were chartered to, or what they were doing." There was a big ledger that all I would have to do was ask the dispatcher where this scow was, and where that scow was, and he would say, "Where was she yesterday?" And I would tell him, because I had the record of where she was yesterday. He would say, "She's still there," or, if she wasn't still there, he would say, "She was sent down to the SS *Augusta* to pick up a cargo of chalk and bring it to the Benjamin-Moore-Carter depot, where they will discharge the cargo." Or another group of scows would be chartered to the New York Central Railroad or to the Delaware, Lackawanna, and Western Railroad or the Erie, or the Jersey Central, or the Brooklyn-Long Island Railroad, whatever.

John T. Mason, Jr.: It was just a little more than being an office boy then?

Admiral Moran: Yes, I was getting along then. The war in Europe had commenced.*

John T. Mason, Jr.: Before you do that—you had started to tell me about getting a license from the Steamboat Inspection Service.

Admiral Moran: I'll get to that later.

John T. Mason, Jr.: Well, the war in Europe had broken out in 1914.

Admiral Moran: Yes, and I was interested in it and anxious to know all of what I could find out about the naval aspect of it. My sympathy was surely with the side of our future allies, and I gave thought, in 1916, to joining the Canadians in the fight. I recall the sinking of the *Lusitania* and was greatly disturbed by it.† I had often seen the ship and had great respect for it and for the people who manned it.

John T. Mason, Jr.: How much contact did you have with the people who manned the *Lusitania*?

Admiral Moran: I only compared them to the people who manned the tugboats. I thought what great people these are who can bring these ships safely back and forth to Europe on a schedule that can be fixed almost to the hour and who can brave the seas and meet all the difficult conditions of navigation and seamanship. I had often seen the commanding officers of these large vessels standing up there with great dignity and assurance.

I was also very much interested in the conduct of my stepfather in handling the work that he would undertake. He never lost what I suppose we would now refer to as poise; he never spoke in a loud voice; he never confused anyone by what he was asking

---

* On 1 August 1914 Germany declared war on Russia and two days later on France. On 4 August German forces invaded Belgium, and that same day Great Britain declared war on Germany. World War I lasted until an armistice was achieved on 11 November 1918.

† On 7 May 1915 a German submarine torpedoed and sank the Cunard Line passenger ship *Lusitania* off the coast of Ireland. All told, 1,198 people died out of the on-board total of 1,924; 128 of the dead were Americans. The event aroused great anger, led to the temporary suspension of the Germans' unrestricted submarine warfare, and was a factor in the 1917 entry into World War I by the United States.

them to do. He always spoke simply. He was very strict; on his tug meals were served to the whole crew by one cook—or steward, as they were called—at one sitting, but no one could start a meal before he was seated at the table. And he spoke very little at the table except at times he wished to persuade someone to change his ways or change his methods. He was never difficult to deal with when he was teaching someone how to do something. He understood the difficulties of learning and the difficulties he had in achieving the position he achieved. So he was a compassionate man in those respects, but he was very dignified. He never used bad language, and he never told a lie. He said to me once he never told a lie. He may have been misunderstood, but he always spoke the truth, and he never used bad language—never.

John T. Mason, Jr.: What a remarkable person.

Admiral Moran: Yes, he was.

John T. Mason, Jr.: And what a great opportunity to grow up under him and to have him interested in you.

Admiral Moran: Yes. Later on, I will tell you about another man who had a great influence on what I have done and my conduct and my behavior. I have been influenced by men I have met, and I have tried to assume the best aspects of their character. I haven't always achieved the result I wanted, but I have always tried, and I've always had in mind, and my conscience would always tell me when I was doing something that my hero wouldn't have done.

John T. Mason, Jr.: Did your mother have the same kind of standards?

Admiral Moran: From this time on, my mother did not influence me very much. I was away a lot of the time. In the summer times, from the time my mother married, I was away with my stepfather.

John T. Mason, Jr.: You were in a man's world, weren't you?

Admiral Moran: I was in a man's world. I had a few summers with an aunt of mine who took me under her wing and looked after me and brought me to a vacation spot on Long Island. She had a great influence on me, because she was a very good woman. My mother was untiring in her effort to manage everything. My stepfather was away; he would be home possibly on Sunday when his tug was here and not engaged, but for the most part he was away until he became older. I would think that he was away until probably 1921 or 1922.

John T. Mason, Jr.: Did they have children?

Admiral Moran: No.
My friends and I frequently discussed our prospective entry into the war against Germany and its allies and were not uncertain about the position we would take as soon as it happened.

John T. Mason, Jr.: You mean that we would get into it?

Admiral Moran: Yes.

John T. Mason, Jr.: Was this a general attitude in New York?

Admiral Moran: Well, the President said that he was going to keep us out of war.[*] When they sank the *Lusitania* and later an American vessel or two, we felt certain as youngsters that we were bound to get into it; we wanted to get in it; we thought it was an unfair thing to do—go around sinking ships and murdering people.

John T. Mason, Jr.: Were there refugees, so to speak, coming into New York Harbor that you had a chance—?

---

[*] Woodrow Wilson was President of the United States from March 1913 to March 1921.

Admiral Moran: No, I never knew that; I never saw that side of it, just saw the newspapers. We kept a chart on the wall in the office—a private little chart—where the armies were, which we would get from the newspapers.

John T. Mason, Jr.: You and the boys your age—your friends were largely in the business, were they?

Admiral Moran: My friends were largely in the business, but I had one particular friend who was in the business of selling food to the shipping lines, and he and I went together to enroll. Early in May, I enrolled in the United States Naval Reserve Force.

John T. Mason, Jr.: How did your family react to that step?

Admiral Moran: My mother was away, and that helped.

John T. Mason, Jr.: How did Mr. Reynolds react?

Admiral Moran: He thought that was just—that war was on—April.* It was May, and I wasn't in it yet.

John T. Mason, Jr.: Youngsters in those days were the same as they are now.

Admiral Moran: Sure. I enlisted as a third class quartermaster. I had difficulty in passing the physical examination but finally, after two trials, succeeded. I think I weighed about 114 pounds.

John T. Mason, Jr.: You were too small.

Admiral Moran: Too small, too light. Was 5-feet-6, but I was very light.

---

*On 6 April 1917 the U.S. Congress declared war on Germany.

John T. Mason, Jr.: What did you do?

Admiral Moran: I really did not know what the difference in duties would be for a quartermaster in the Navy, as compared to the duties of the quartermaster in the commercial field of shipping. I was so pleased to be enrolled that I was unconcerned about the rating or the duties of the rating. One of my earliest assignments was with a group known as the "break-down gang," whose particular job it was to relieve a merchant ship crew on a ship which the Navy had taken to operate in the naval service.

John T. Mason, Jr.: How did the Navy arrive at taking a ship like that? Was it through the War Shipping Board?

Admiral Moran: It was done probably by the United States Maritime Commission in those days, or what was known as the United States Shipping Board. It was the predecessor of the War Shipping Administration or now, the Maritime Administration.

The vessels were taken to meet the logistic needs and most generally vessels of cargo capacities required by the Navy, and passenger vessels for transportation of troops.

John T. Mason, Jr.: So there was a need for a temporary kind of crew?

Admiral Moran: Yes. The Navy-acquired merchant ship was taken and brought by the break-down crew to a shipyard, a naval base, a loading berth, or another port for whatever needs. The trip or the tour would be a week, or three at most. The total operation was under the command of Lieutenant Commander R. T. Merrill and was known as the Naval Overseas Transportation Service.*

John T. Mason, Jr.: Now, this was all confined to the East Coast, was it?

---

* Lieutenant Commander Robert T. Merrill, USN. See Lewis P. Clephane, *History of the Naval Overseas Transportation Service in World War I* (Washington: Naval History Division, 1969).

Admiral Moran: Based at the south end of Manhattan Island. This was then confined or restricted to the East Coast, so far as I know. It was not, to the best of my knowledge, then organized on the West Coast, because there was no war activity in the Pacific at that time or later in that war.

John T. Mason, Jr.: Are you going to tell me how far afield you went as a member of this temporary crew?

Admiral Moran: The break-down gang consisted of about 30 enlisted men and eight officers, all but a few of whom were merchant mariners. Since many of the ships the Navy took to operate were acquired in New York, I was somewhat helpful to the deck officers in my knowledge of the port and its geography, tidal conditions, and channel depths. This information was made known to one of the officers of the group—to the assignment officer in NOTS, who sent for me to discuss the possibility of my becoming an officer in the gang. The gang consisted of experienced men as watch officers on deck, engineering officers, seamen and boatswain's mates, stewards, and cooks. I was a seaman, a quartermaster. I steered the ship under orders from the officer of the deck, and I would keep the wheelhouse in order and all of its gear in order and deliver my part of my duties to the succeeding permanent quartermaster third class.

John T. Mason, Jr.: But you were equipped with this very special knowledge of New York Harbor.

Admiral Moran: That's right. I could help the officers, and I would be able to tell the officer who was standing in front of me what to do. When he would see a vessel approaching us, he would say, "Which way do you think that fellow is going?" or "Where is he bound?" or "What's the set of the tide here?" or "What's that place over there?" "Which berth are we going to?" He would ask those questions, and I could respond and help. But where I was weak was in transmitting signals—hand signals by semaphore or at night by blinkers. I didn't know the Morse code well, and I didn't know the semaphore signals well. And I didn't know the flag-hoist signals well, which some of the regular fellows knew immediately.

But I did know the business of getting around a ship and helping to a greater extent than quartermasters would generally help, because I had this experience from running around here and running up and down the coast. I was a good judge of distance too. A fellow would say to me, "How far away are we? How much room do we have in there?" or "How close are we to that vessel coming?" I knew the distances, and I could relate the distance from the land to the water with relatively no difficulty.

He questioned me and decided that I was probably material as a deck officer, but I lacked naval vessel operation and customs, and it would not be fair to me or others to have me commissioned without more knowledge of the naval officer's duties afloat. So he had me assigned to the Pelham Bay Officers' Training School, on the understanding what I would return to NOTS service at the end of two months, when, if I met the requirements of the course, would be commissioned an ensign. There was no intention of my going to Pelham for the course for any other purpose but to come back to this thing I had been doing, but to come back as an officer.

John T. Mason, Jr.: To be equipped with the naval knowledge that you lacked.

Admiral Moran: To be equipped with the naval knowledge, because when the naval crews would come aboard the ship, they would ask me questions that would grow out of their need to know where on a merchant ship this would be, or how on a merchant ship that would be done. I was unacquainted with what the people were talking about when they would come and ask those questions and ask for the procedures on the flag-hoist arrangements and the semaphore and the blinker systems. I had some difficulty with gunnery. They taught me a little at Pelham, and naval practices and customs.

John T. Mason, Jr.: Also the Morse code, did they teach you, and communications?

Admiral Moran: Oh, sure. After a discussion with the head of the course, I was commissioned and sent back to South Ferry, to Commander Merrill's office, for further orders.

John T. Mason, Jr.: Would you tell me a little about that school at Pelham Manor? Was that set up because of the fact that we were getting into the war?

Admiral Moran: We were in the war. It was an officers' training school, and they used to call the graduates 90-day wonders or something like that, and they used to get them out. All the fellows were from academic education, quick learners, but they had very little or practically no practical experience. They were sent to sea on merchant ships for training, I think for a month, and they got the hang of the way a merchant ship was operated. They went on not as officers but just as observers. They came back and took the course in navigation, gunnery, communications, ship management.

The first assignment I got when I went out of there was to learn the method of preparing gear to cut mine cables. The ships were equipped with a fitting. The forefoot was the bottom of the stem of the bow of the ship, and cables were attached to it and gears which could be towed and spread from the stem of the ship to cut and entangle the wires of floating mines; the fittings were called otter gears. I first went to learn how to instruct deck officers in the fitting and equipping of those gears.

John T. Mason, Jr.: They were new?

Admiral Moran: They were brand new.

John T. Mason, Jr.: Born of the experience that the British were having with the mines?

Admiral Moran: That's right. The situation there at NOTS, Commander Merrill's office, changed somewhat, to the extent that the activity of the break-down crew had declined, and a shortage had arisen for officers in the overseas aspect of their operations. By the time I got out—in the two months I was away at Pelham—NOTS had acquired all of the merchant ships that were available to the Navy. The newly built ships were coming out, and there was a shortage of officers there.

John T. Mason, Jr.: I can see where one job diminished and the other one grew.

Admiral Moran: Right. When I learned of this condition, I approached my stepfather, who was in the business of handling ships for the Navy around the harbor here and taking them on coastwise pilotage trips, going from here to Norfolk or to Philadelphia or to Boston or to Portland, Maine, or to Halifax. He would become acquainted with masters of these vessels, and they would discuss with him the operation of the ships and where they were going and the officers they had on the ships, the ones who were good and those who weren't so good—not entirely incompetent but unaccustomed or untrained properly for the jobs. My father handled, as a harbor and coastwise pilot, naval vessels and never failed to exhibit great skill and disposition, as I have told you.

He found a new ship in need of a deck officer, capable of standing a junior watch, and made an appointment for me to see its commanding officer, Lieutenant Commander Nicholas Fogarty, a former chief officer in the Matson Line of San Francisco.

John T. Mason, Jr.: He was a reservist too?

Admiral Moran: He was a reservist and was then commanding the USS *Passaic*, a refrigerator ship of about 6,000 deadweight tons. Captain Fogarty looked me over, asked a few questions, and concluded that beggars can't be choosers.

Have you got anything on that?

John T. Mason, Jr.: Yes, she was commissioned on 2 July 1918 and renamed the *Ice King*.

Admiral Moran: The ship was commissioned USS *Passaic* and renamed *Ice King*, but no one told the captain of the ship or anybody else that his vessel had been renamed. So we loaded a cargo of beef in Hoboken, New Jersey, and we went to Bordeaux, discharged the beef, loaded again, and went to St. Nazaire, discharged the cargo, came back again. When we came in the Narrows, we came by the duty ship there.* They signaled over to us that our name had been changed two trips ago. We were reporting the USS *Passaic*, and they said, "Your name is not *Passaic*; it is *Ice King*." So we then found out our name.†

John T. Mason, Jr.: What was the reason for the change?

Admiral Moran: I guess the vessel didn't rate a name after a city as large as Passaic, New Jersey. I think that was it, or else Passaic didn't think they ought to have a refrigerator ship named for it.

John T. Mason, Jr.: And *Ice King* seemed more appropriate for a reefer ship.

Admiral Moran: Yes, because we were really *Ice King*.

John T. Mason, Jr.: Tell me about some of those voyages to Europe. How long did it take to cross the Atlantic?

Admiral Moran: I received orders to join the vessel and did so promptly. We shifted from the fitting-out berth to Hoboken, New Jersey, where we took on about 4,500 tons of frozen beef for Bordeaux.

John T. Mason, Jr.: Was this U.S. beef?

Admiral Moran: I presume so. The voyage outbound was completed after a number of discouraging events and mishaps, but I was afforded an opportunity to demonstrate a

---

* This is a reference to the Verrazano Narrows between Brooklyn and Staten Island.
† The Navy's official history of the ship indicates that her name was changed shortly before she was commissioned. The *Ice King* was 392 feet long, 52 feet in the beam, had a maximum draft of 24 feet, displacement of 10,562 tons, and a maximum speed of 10 knots.

willingness to work longer and more diligently than was expected and was commended for the effort.

Everything happened. First, we left Hoboken, proceeded down the North River, up the East River, through Long Island Sound to a point off Port Jefferson, where the coastwise pilot received word from the engine room that the steering engine had broken down. So we anchored, and the steering engine was fixed.

John T. Mason, Jr.: A sitting duck, though; weren't there submarines out there?

Admiral Moran: No, not in Long Island Sound. That was guarded by gates. We resumed the voyage. We were bound for North Sydney, Cape Breton Island, where we were to join a convoy coming out of the Great Lakes, for France. That involved a passage outside of Cape Cod and coastwise to Nova Scotia, without escort.

John T. Mason, Jr.: What was your speed?

Admiral Moran: Nine or ten knots. The morning after the breakdown of the steering engine, we were approaching Cape Cod when we grounded in the fog. Captain Fogarty was very displeased with the pilot; it was a very embarrassing thing for him. It was his first command in the Navy, and here his ship was on the bottom.

John T. Mason, Jr.: But it had been under the control of the pilot?

Admiral Moran: The coastwise pilot was supposed to know the area. He was put there to keep Captain Fogarty out of trouble. Instead, he got him into trouble. We anchored so we wouldn't shift further ashore. The fog lifted about noontime, and the visibility was sufficient for us to get under way, so the captain ordered that the anchor be raised. I was on the forecastle head with the executive officer of the ship. I was watching the anchor come up, and I saw that a shackle, on breaking the water, had spread, and the shackle bolt (pin) was out of the eye. The chain was very likely to slip out of the open shackle, so I called for the executive officer to stop heaving and report the incident to the bridge. He did that, and we put a boatswain's mate over the bow and secured the chain between the anchor and the shackle so that we wouldn't lose it. We hove in the chain and then hove in the anchor on the line we fastened to it and got under way.

The captain discharged the pilot to a ship, unknown to me, going into Boston. We proceeded without pilotage to Halifax and on the way discovered that we had a broken valve stem guide on the high-pressure cylinder of the engine.

John T. Mason, Jr.: Was that due to the grounding?

Admiral Moran: No. The captain sent me down, after the engineer reported to him, to the engine room to look at the valve stem and report to him what I saw. And he asked me to do it as discreetly as possible—as though I were interested in knowing only about the valve stem guide. He had some doubts about the necessity for going in to make the repair. I went down to the engine room and asked the chief engineer to show me the valve stem guide. And he said, "Why do you want to see the valve stem guide?"

I said, "Just for my education, I'd like to see it."

He said, "You're not going to know any more after you have seen it than before, but come with me." So we climbed up on the grating, and I saw the crack in the valve stem guide. I thanked him for having shown it to me, and I went back and reported to the captain. He knew no more than I did about the need for replacing it. In any event, he decided that he would take the ship into Halifax and see if we could get the repair done. We did, and we got the repair done.

We proceeded to Cape Breton Island. The convoy was coming out of the St. Lawrence and would be there the next day. We had missed the original convoy; this was a new one coming out, and we joined it. We arrived off Sydney about 2:00 o'clock in the morning, and the harbor was closed. There was a chain across the mouth of the harbor. The captain left the bridge, and the watch officer left the bridge, and he left me up there alone with the ship. And he said, "You're bright enough to keep out of trouble. Just stay off here until daybreak and call me. Don't come close to any passing vessels; keep a good lookout." So I ran the ship offshore a little bit, came back again, did it again, and day broke about 4:00 or 4:30, daylight. I called the captain, and we went in. We got a pilot; the pilot boat came out and brought us in.

Halfway across the Atlantic—this ship was a coal burner—we had a fire in the main coal bunker. So we had to take all the coal out of the coal bunker to get to the burning coal, cool it off, then put it back.

John T. Mason, Jr.: Did this require the cooperation of the whole crew?

Admiral Moran: Everybody, but I was more industrious than most guys.

John T. Mason, Jr.: You did a lot of shoveling.

Admiral Moran: I got a lot of shoveling all right. We had a good escort in the convoy across the Atlantic. I think there were probably 35 ships in the convoy, and we were zigzagging all the time at about ten knots. It was a ten-knot convoy of low-powered ships.

John T. Mason, Jr.: How many escorts did you have?

Admiral Moran: I think we had two destroyers on each side.

We arrived at the point where the convoy would split—those going to Great Britain and those going south to France. There was then a good deal of confusion. I was called upon to deal with the communications aspect of the problems that were arising, because our captain was named the deputy convoy commander, and he had charge of this group going south. We straightened it out, and we proceeded into Brest to prepare for new coastwise escorts. Coastwise escort consisted of a fishing trawler towing a balloon. We were halfway down between St. Nazaire and Brest, and it was nearly 12:00 o'clock noon. I had the gun watch on the forward gun when a submarine was reported outside of us by the convoy fellow, and a torpedo was seen coming towards us. Fortunately, the torpedo missed its mark, and we proceeded along for ten minutes or so when the ship astern of us was hit, and she blew up. She had a deck load of lumber, and lumber was flying all over the place. We fired at what we thought was the submarine, but we saw no result from the firing.

John T. Mason, Jr.: What kind of guns did you have?

Admiral Moran: We had a 6-inch gun aft and a 3-inch gun forward on the forecastle head. We fired both of them. General quarters and all the rest of it. We got into St. Nazaire and then to Bordeaux without any further trouble. We got in there and discharged our cargo, and I think we were about a week in port. And we came back here to New York without anything further happening.

John T. Mason, Jr.: How did the crew react to being under attack from a submarine?

Admiral Moran: Everyone was acting the same way, scared stiff but carrying on. If we had seen the submarine, we would have hit her. We didn't see it; we had only the faintest idea where the wake of the torpedo came. We shot out in the range of that. We had to be careful we didn't hit any other ships. We had no protection at all from the trawler. The trawler just told us he got a signal from the balloon that there was a submarine out there.

John T. Mason, Jr.: What did the balloon accomplish—just observation?

Admiral Moran: Yes.

John T. Mason, Jr.: How was the crew received in Bordeaux when you were there? You unloaded your cargo, and you were there for a week or so.

Admiral Moran: While I refer to Bordeaux, actually the location of the discharging area was at a place called Bascennes, south of Bordeaux. It was an area created for the purpose of receiving logistics in whatever form they came, and it was sparsely populated. The town had nothing that I could notice. The crews were given liberty and went to Bordeaux, which, as I remember, was maybe five or six miles above Bascennes. The stevedores were American Army men, and the unloading was done under normal conditions at a foreign port. There was nothing unusual about it.

John T. Mason, Jr.: Were there temporary warehouses there?

Admiral Moran: Temporary warehouses, and much of the cargo was loaded into French railway cars—refrigerated cars—and taken to their ultimate destination.

John T. Mason, Jr.: What did the *Ice King* do in the way of ballast on the way back? Did you take anything back?

Admiral Moran: We loaded ballast. It was a very, very difficult task. We tried hard to get more than we were allowed, because the ship was light of coal; we didn't take any coal aboard. We got some sand and some rocks. It put us down, I think, to a mean draft of 20 feet, which was not bad considering the time of year we were making passage to the west. The first trip was a relatively smooth trip home.

John T. Mason, Jr.: Did you have any kind of escort as you left the French port?

Admiral Moran: We left the French port, and we were escorted out to 50 degrees west longitude.

John T. Mason, Jr.: Wasn't that the dangerous area where the submarines were operating?

Admiral Moran: We might have been escorted to 50 west.

John T. Mason, Jr.: So you got back to New York. Did you reload immediately?

Admiral Moran: We reloaded immediately.

John T. Mason, Jr.: Same kind of cargo?

Admiral Moran: Same kind of cargo; same place. Then we made another trip and another trip.

John T. Mason, Jr.: In the meantime you had been made an ensign.

Admiral Moran: Yes, and I was promoted at the end of the second trip to lieutenant (junior grade). At the end of the second trip, which occurred in November, I received orders to proceed to the West Coast with Captain Fogarty to get a new ship and come back to the East Coast. We got to the West Coast, I think, on Thanksgiving Day, reported to the NOTS at the West Coast personnel office, and were told that the ship we were to take was not ready.

John T. Mason, Jr.: Where were you picking her up?

Admiral Moran: Moore Shipyard, San Francisco. But by this time the Armistice had been signed, and there was a great doubt in the officers' minds that we would ever get out.[*] But we were kept there at San Francisco until after Christmas. A day or two after Christmas—I've forgotten exactly when it was—we were told that our services were not needed, and we were ordered to return to New York for further orders. I got here in New York and was assigned to a ship called the USS *Yellowstone*, which had railway material in her—locomotives, tracks, all kinds of machinery—for France.[†] The ship was in a berth at Brooklyn Army Base. We laid there through January, and in February my people here, my uncles, were anxious to have me back, and they took some steps, unknown to me, to have me placed on inactive duty. And that was the end of my career in the First World War.

---

[*] The Armistice that ended World War I in Europe went into effect on 11 November 1918.

[†] The single-screw freighter *War Boy* was completed in 1918 on the West Coast. After she had steamed to the East Coast, the Navy acquired her at Philadelphia for operation as part of the Naval Overseas Transportation Service. She was commissioned as the USS *Yellowstone* on 21 September 1918. The ship displaced 12,570 tons, was 416 feet long, 53 feet in the beam, had a mean draft of 34 feet, and a top speed of ten knots.

John T. Mason, Jr.: Were you glad to come back, or did you want some more service with the Navy?

Admiral Moran: I was making more money in the Navy than I was making in the office. That was somewhat of a controlling factor, but I knew that my future would not be in the Navy—or I didn't expect it to be, at least. I could foresee all of these naval officers being discharged, and I thought I might as well go. I knew quite a few fellows who had not been in the service I was in who had come out; they had been discharged, and the Navy was glad to see the end of them. Their vessels were laid up—submarine chasers and little escort vessels and yachts and so forth.

John T. Mason, Jr.: What was the atmosphere at that point? Was it similar to what happened after World War II—everybody wanting to get out at once?

Admiral Moran: Yes, I expect so. I was less sophisticated about that sort of thing. I was only interested in going to sea. I had some good results with Captain Fogarty in my trips with him. He was very anxious for his officers to become proficient as quickly as they could be and under the conditions that they were working. He had two junior officers, and he insisted upon them doing celestial navigation. And he wanted their reports before the convoy commodore asked for the position reports every day at noon. He wanted to have his first, because his navigator was a very good navigator. He didn't want our reports to be relied upon. He wanted us to report before the others did, because he was worried that we might be influenced by the other reports.

John T. Mason, Jr.: He wanted you to acquire this on your own.

Admiral Moran: Right. He said that he was going to give one of us a day's liberty in France for the fellow with the best record of position reports for the voyage. It was awful close. We didn't confer when we took noon sights, working out the position. But it was so close that he couldn't decide, so I suggested to him that he decide on the basis of nationality.

John T. Mason, Jr.: The other fellow being what?

Admiral Moran: A Swede. "No," he said, "I'll give it to you both."

John T. Mason, Jr.: Where had you acquired your knowledge of celestial navigation? Here at Pelham?

Admiral Moran: No, I did most of it—I went to the Seaman's Church Institute.

John T. Mason, Jr.: When did you do that?

Admiral Moran: I did that before I went in the Navy. The simplest kind of things—longitude sight and latitude sight. We didn't do any stars; we weren't supposed to do any stars. We would take a position at 4:00 o'clock, and we would adjust the compass too. We had a standard compass, and we did the best we could with it.

John T. Mason, Jr.: When you came back to the company as a jaygee, you were of a more senior rank, so what happened?* You must have gotten a better job.

Admiral Moran: My senior uncle, Eugene Moran, went in the Navy at the outset of the break of war, and he established a minesweeping force for the commandant of the Brooklyn Navy Yard. He was away for six or eight months, I guess, from the office. My junior uncle was alone here, and he had the burden of running the company before my senior uncle returned after the minesweeping force was dismissed. My senior uncle also had to do with the acquisition and outfitting of yachts for operation on the British and French coasts against submarines. He came back, and the two of them were running the company, and I had been out since 1917. It was now 1919, so I came in and found a spot

---

* Jaygee—lieutenant (junior grade).

for myself in the operating phase of the business, which wasn't a great task then, because it was a relatively small company.

John T. Mason, Jr.: I assume, however, that it had grown in World War I. I mean, the activity in the New York Harbor was much greater.

Admiral Moran: Oh yes, it had grown some. I worked on development plans, expansion plans, and I was given a free hand too. Anybody that was willing to work long hours without complaint, glad to do it, was given an opportunity. Business was expanding; the whole country was expanding. It was a great opportunity, and everybody did well. Things were pretty good.

John T. Mason, Jr.: Had your experience with the Navy broadened your vision? Then you could apply this to your own tugboat business?

Admiral Moran: Surely. These fellows knew I was a navigating officer in the *Ice King* for the last trip I made in it, and they felt I was fairly hot stuff.

John T. Mason, Jr.: You were too. What kind of plans did you develop for expansion? What did you think of in terms of the company?

Admiral Moran: I rather think that I was more concerned about the company's profitability. I was wondering what the most profitable area for the company in the world of New York Harbor would be. I did everything—acted as purchasing agent; I was interested in reducing the risk of accidents and damage. Insurance appealed to me; I was anxious to get insurance rates down. I did everything I could in the operating phase to get the company profitable. Because it was the kind of company that I think was relied upon by the people who ran it for the net profit, rather than thinking in terms of the shareholders. The competition we had was composed of companies owned by individuals who didn't think in respect of benefits for others. It was just run for their own business, a private operation.

It was like the captain coming ashore; he was getting the same pay or a little bit more—or if it earned more or he could find ways to expand. In 1906 this company was organized as a corporation with stock, and the shareholders hadn't seen much in the way of dividends for 10 or 12 years. I thought in terms of how we ought to change its course. I saw the profitable areas, or what appeared to be profitable areas, and I concentrated on them and succeeded to a degree.

John T. Mason, Jr.: This meant launching out into new phases. What new phases did you develop?

Admiral Moran: I thought that the handling of ships was particularly profitable. The company had, during the war, handled ships for the Navy, but it wasn't a profitable operation.

John T. Mason, Jr.: It never is with a government contract.

Admiral Moran: No, that's right. In addition to that, you had a wartime atmosphere. People were, "Let's win the war, and don't be bothered so much about the rates as long as you're getting even and meeting your payroll and your expenses." I really finally developed that until we were really the biggest in the place. Then I also felt that the coastwise towing business promised a good profit.

John T. Mason, Jr.: What did that entail?

Admiral Moran: Well, that entailed towing ships from one place to another—disabled ships, dredges, car floats, barges laden with coal, oil barges, petroleum barges between here and Providence, Boston, Philadelphia. We towed a concrete car float from New York to Key West; we towed a ship from here to the port of Caracas. We did lots of things like that. We did rescue work in a smaller way. The next series—the series on the time from 1922 to 1924—we started to expand, and we expanded until we really were the best.

John T. Mason, Jr.: What sort of competition did you have in those early postwar days?

Admiral Moran: We had competition from a lot of companies which were operated by older men whose ambition had decreased, whose needs had decreased. And there weren't too many younger people such as I who were attracted to this business. So, truthfully, I would think that the reason I had as much luck as I did was because I was competing with people who didn't need to do that sort of thing, were satisfied with what they had. As long as we didn't take too much from them, they thought it was all right. They'd get something.

John T. Mason, Jr.: I see some of your grandfather's spirit cropping up in you.

Admiral Moran: I rather think that's right too.

Interview Number 2 with Rear Admiral Edmond J. Moran, U.S. Naval Reserve (Retired)
Place: Admiral Moran's office in the World Trade Center, New York City
Date: Wednesday, 8 June 1977
Interviewer: John T. Mason, Jr.

John T. Mason, Jr.: Admiral, as you know, it is a delight to be with you and always an inspiration. Today, I think, perhaps you want to deal with the kind of advice the Navy called upon you to render at various times in the '30s and again after your period of service in World War II. Perhaps the first incident—at least the one I have knowledge of—is in the late 1930s when you helped the Navy design a fleet ocean tug.

Admiral Moran: That's correct.

John T. Mason, Jr.: How did that come about?

Admiral Moran: I was, at that time, interested in the hull construction and the machinery of the prospective salvage tugs. The Navy had made inquiries with respect to the hull, as to deck fittings, towing apparatus, navigational equipment, the power plant, and propulsion machinery.

John T. Mason, Jr.: This was BuShips who made the inquiries?

Admiral Moran: This was the Bureau of Ships. The Navy had adopted the diesel-electric drive for the kind of tug that they proposed to build. I thought this propulsion, while expensive to acquire and operate, would prove to be very desirable with regard to handling and general maintenance. The vessels could turn their propellers through the electric drive as low as four or five revolutions and up to 200 revolutions. This flexibility was important in diesel power, and the Navy was right in the decision to standardize at that time on this equipment. In respect to the deck department and the layout of the house structure on the main deck and the pilothouse structure on the upper deck and the fitting of lights and equipment for passing signals and rules—compliance with rules to prevent collisions—their system was very good indeed. The ships, the tugs, were built on the East Coast and on the lakes and turned out very satisfactorily.

John T. Mason, Jr.: How many were they in the process of getting?

Admiral Moran: I do not recall how many there were. I was able to go on trial trips of one or two of the vessels, and they performed very well indeed.

John T. Mason, Jr.: The Navy called upon you, I assume, because you had become an expert in this area. Had you not dieselized, so to speak, your own tugs?

Admiral Moran: We had started a dieselization program, but our experience with respect to diesel machinery in propulsion was more in the area of investigation and comparison. We thought that the best diesel engine at the time was made by the Winton Engine Company in Cleveland, but this machinery was four cycle, and that resulted in more weight than we thought desirable. So when the decision with respect to the ATFs was under consideration, the General Motors Company, which had acquired the Winton Engine Company—they were automobile manufacturers in the early days—the General Motors engineering people, including Mr. Kettering, felt that the two-cycle engine of much higher speed would be more economical and of considerably less weight.[*] It was on the basis of this information and the studies which were made by the Navy's Bureau of Ships and our technical people that the two-cycle, high-speed engine was adopted for the ATFs. The machinery operated to form the power for the electric motors which turned the propellers.

John T. Mason, Jr.: Did you have any particular contact in the Bureau of Ships at that time? Did you work with any particular man down there?

---

[*] ATF is the Navy designation for an oceangoing fleet tug. Charles F. Kettering was an electrical engineer and manufacturer. He was president of General Motors Research Corporation and vice president of the General Motors Corporation. He invented a number of systems for cars.

Admiral Moran: I can't recall.

John T. Mason, Jr.: Was that the first instance when the Navy called upon you for technical advice?

Admiral Moran: Yes.

John T. Mason, Jr.: And when was the next time they did?

Admiral Moran: The next time I heard from the Navy, I heard from Commander Mumma; I think he was a commander at the time.* He was fitting out or working on plans for a tug which would be known as ATR, a rescue tug, and there were many problems connected with the design and construction of this equipment, because the vessels were to be of wood in the main at the outset because of the lack of steel. So I was able to help in much the same way as I tried to help in connection with the ATFs.

John T. Mason, Jr.: Was this also before we got into World War II?

Admiral Moran: This might have been just before or just immediately after.† It is hard for me to think back as to the exact time. I was also able to help in connection with the construction of the smaller ATF, which was built and known as the ATA.‡ This tug was designed by Thames, Incorporated, which became a General Motors subsidiary. At the outset it was privately owned, and the architect was a man named Robert Cook. He designed the ATA to meet British requirements, and some of the early vessels were built for and delivered to the British. They were very satisfactory, of considerably less power than the ATFs but suitable for ocean towing, and their principal asset was that they required a much smaller crew than the ATF. Seagoing tug crews were becoming scarce

---

* This is a reference to Lieutenant Commander Albert G. Mumma, USN, an engineering duty specialist who served in the Bureau of Ships in the early 1940s. The oral history of Mumma, who later became a rear admiral, is in the Naval Institute oral history collection.
† The U.S. Congress declared war on Japan on 8 December 1941, one day after the Japanese attack on U.S. Navy ships at Pearl Harbor, Hawaii.
‡ ATA is the Navy designation for an auxiliary tug.

in Great Britain, as well as on the Atlantic Coast, and for that reason these tugs were desirable. They had good sea-keeping qualities, and they, too, were high-speed electric drives with good endurance so far as fuel was concerned.

John T. Mason, Jr.: If they were oceangoing, they would have to, wouldn't they?

Admiral Moran: They were in some demand when they became surplus at the end of World War II, both here and abroad.

John T. Mason, Jr.: How numerous were they?

Admiral Moran: I would think that there were probably 50 built, and they were built in yards in quantity so as to cheapen the cost on a quantitative basis.

John T. Mason, Jr.: These are private yards, I guess.

Admiral Moran: Yes, private yards.

John T. Mason, Jr.: And your contribution was in your expertise?

Admiral Moran: In outfitting and in estimating crew requirements, placement of deck fittings, and general layout.

John T. Mason, Jr.: Another instance I know about is in 1967, when you contributed to the Navy design of the salvage ship, the ATS.

Admiral Moran: My interest in that vessel was to the extent that it was fitted for towing as well as for salvage operations. I made no contribution at all with respect to the gear, the hull arrangement, or its stowage capacity for salvage gear.

John T. Mason, Jr.: It was the rescue aspect.

Admiral Moran: It was the rescue aspect, the towing qualities, and its type of propeller. The propeller that it would be fitted for would necessarily take into account the pitch and revolutions it would accommodate in heavy towing or light towing, as well as in running without a tow.

John T. Mason, Jr.: When the Navy called upon you for that kind of advice, did you have to sign a contract with them?

Admiral Moran: No. Whenever I gave any advice, I neither received nor asked for any compensation. This was all gratis.

John T. Mason, Jr.: That was indeed generous. It was demanding on your time, wasn't it?

Admiral Moran: My time wasn't all that important.

John T. Mason, Jr.: Tell me about the events in the early '60s, when the Navy, in towing, lost a number of ships that they were bringing out of reserve.

Admiral Moran: The first incident that I can recall was the loss of a destroyer on the Jersey coast, whilst in tow of an ATA.[*] The destroyer broke away from the tug and wound up on the beach.

John T. Mason, Jr.: This must have been embarrassing to the Navy.

Admiral Moran: It was, but the difficulty was in the assignment of personnel to the job the tug was assigned to do. The commander of the Eastern Sea Frontier called upon us to

---

[*] In March 1962, the decommissioned destroyer *Monssen* (DD-798) was being towed down the East Coast to the reserve fleet at Philadelphia. On 6 March the towline to the destroyer parted in high winds and heavy seas. The *Monssen* went aground at Beach Haven Inlet, New Jersey, and remained there for six days before being pulled off and completing the original trip.

confer with them with respect to the towage problems with which he was confronted. There was no question at all about the suitability or the fitness of the tugs the Navy proposed to use for the service intended. There was great doubt in our minds as to the suitability or the fitness and experience of the commanding officer and the crew of the tug.

John T. Mason, Jr.: Does this say that the Navy underestimated the problems involved in towing? Did they fail to appreciate that?

Admiral Moran: It said to us that there was a lack of awareness as to the requirement of the deck officers of the tugs as to the requirements of their positions. They had never, in some cases, undertaken towages that they were called upon to make, and they were at a loss to do what they might have done, or an experienced tug man would have done in the positions of difficulty which they found themselves in. It was simply that a meeting of the commanding officers of these tugs was held, and questions they raised were answered, and advice given as to what to do under standard, somewhat difficult positions in which they found themselves.

John T. Mason, Jr.: Now, do I take it that you ran this meeting?

Admiral Moran: The meeting was run by the commander of the Eastern Sea Frontier, but we were those who were questioned and upon whom the commander of the Eastern Sea Frontier relied for replies and responses and advice.

John T. Mason, Jr.: As you reflect on it, I mean the questions that you were asked—were they the proper ones? Were they ones that would impart the kind of knowledge they should have?

Admiral Moran: The questions they asked were intelligent and based upon their otherwise experience. These men had been engaged in towing targets, running distances, navigation, and operation of the equipment. The tugs themselves were very well looked after, very well cared for, and the commanding officers and the deck officers were more than willing to absorb any advice that they considered helpful in carrying out their duties. They were not in any way reluctant to make inquiries and to accept advice. They made no pretense at all at excusing themselves for anything which they did not successfully carry out in the past.

John T. Mason, Jr.: Was any suggestion made, inasmuch as the Navy does maintain all sorts of schools for various aspects of navigation, that perhaps they should have a school to teach the techniques of towing.

Admiral Moran: The suggestion was made that we would be very pleased to take any deck officers anywhere we went to allow them to observe the methods which we had adopted and the plans for securing the best weather forecasts and the best routes to follow after having received such reports.

John T. Mason, Jr.: Was this offer taken up?

Admiral Moran: Yes, we did take some of the commanding officers, but after we had them they were transferred and given tasks which did not in any way benefit them for the next assignment.

John T. Mason, Jr.: That sounds like the Navy. As a result of this, I am told, the Navy wrote a towing manual, and you had a voice in that.

Admiral Moran: Yes, we did. We read the manual, and we made suggestions with respect to it which, I understand, were followed. We have seen nothing of the manual since.

John T. Mason, Jr.: There was more than one incident, was there not, in that period of time? I mean, there was the destroyer lost on the Jersey coast, but weren't there several others.

Admiral Moran: There were other occurrences which resulted in failure to complete voyages properly and safely without damage. We were asked, in a discreet way, not to think in terms of what had gone before. We were asked to have consideration only for what we might do to avoid future difficulties.

John T. Mason, Jr.: In a case like that, where an officer lost his tow, did they follow the ordinary Navy regulations? Was there a board of inquiry and that sort of thing?

Admiral Moran: I don't know. I never heard about that, nor did we have any interest in that. We were simply trying to help prevent anything that happened to recur.

John T. Mason, Jr.: You say you cannot recall other instances where the Navy called upon you for technical advice, but the Army did, so tell me about those.

Admiral Moran: The Army had designed and built a very large DUKW.[*] It was at San Francisco when it was delivered and was to be towed to Monterey Bay, where it was to be let go by the tug and navigate itself ashore. The trip from San Francisco commenced during fair weather, but on the way the weather changed rapidly and became entirely unsuitable for the DUKW being towed at the rate it had been towed from the start of its departure from San Francisco. It was lost, and the crew with it, on its arrival in the proximity of Monterey Bay. The Army was under considerable criticism for the loss of this valuable piece of equipment and the lives of the two men.

John T. Mason, Jr.: I suppose there was much publicity on it.

Admiral Moran: There wasn't as much as you might think. There was some, but it didn't amount to anything which attracted attention anywhere but in the vicinity of the California coast. I was able to study—

---

[*] DUKW was the designation of an amphibious truck used by the U.S. Army in World War II. The name was pronounced like that of an animal capable of operating on both water and land, the duck. Essentially the DUKW was a boat with wheels on the bottom.

John T. Mason, Jr.: They called you out there?

Admiral Moran: The Army asked me to make a report to them on the incident and account, if possible, for the loss. I looked at all the records I could find, discussed the weather, the manner of towing, the time of departure and the loss, estimated speed over the route, and reported that the vessel had been towed during bad weather at an unreasonably high rate of speed and was simply overcome and swamped. It was believed that the two men on the craft had not properly secured the deck openings to prevent the entrance of water, which swamped the vessel at the high rate it was proceeding.

John T. Mason, Jr.: Was the crew on the tug of considerable help in your analysis of the situation?

Admiral Moran: I was not able to speak to the crew of the tug. I only read reports they had made and took records of the weather over the route, the times of their passing established points of reference.

John T. Mason, Jr.: All of this entailed being on the West Coast?

Admiral Moran: It did.

John T. Mason, Jr.: You said that on other occasions the Army also asked you to go on trial runs?

Admiral Moran: Yes, I have been very frequently asked to attend trial trips for Army tugs, their small craft, and render an opinion as to the suitability of the equipment, and the vessel's condition as compared to the specifications of the vessel's construction.

John T. Mason, Jr.: How often do you find defects that need to be remedied when you do this sort of thing?

Admiral Moran: I have found it generally to be true that the vessels have been built according to the specifications. In some cases the specifications have not been suitable for the purpose the vessel has been intended to serve.

John T. Mason, Jr.: If the vessel is built according to specifications given them, and these are inadequate for the task at hand, then what happens?

Admiral Moran: I simply recommend alterations or improvement in the vessel's fittings, but I have no responsibility towards their being carried out.

John T. Mason, Jr.: Where would you undergo these trial runs? Was there any specific place where this is done?

Admiral Moran: Yes, I have been in Virginia, Charleston, Savannah, and Massachusetts at various shipyards.

John T. Mason, Jr.: All of which you know so thoroughly.

Admiral Moran: I knew well enough.

Interview Number 3 with Rear Admiral Edmond J. Moran, U.S. Naval Reserve (Retired)
Place: Admiral Moran's office in the World Trade Center, New York City
Date: Friday, 7 October 1977
Interviewer: John T. Mason, Jr.

John T. Mason, Jr.: Admiral, I have been looking forward to this interview for quite a long time. We're going to begin to cover your contribution in World War II. It is my understanding that in 1941—and I don't have the date—as a civilian you joined the Maritime Commission as a special assistant in charge of acquisitions of small craft for the Army and the Navy and the British. Would you please tell me the circumstances surrounding that, sir?

Admiral Moran: During the spring of 1941, I was approached by Mr. Huntington T. Morse, who was Admiral Land's assistant.* He was seeking to obtain assistance in the requisition of small craft for the Army and the Navy, and later for the British, who had been subject to serious damage as a result of the blitz. A very great number of their harbor craft and facilities had been damaged by enemy aircraft, and they were shortened to such an extent that some of the ports were unable properly to function. The Navy was looking for patrol craft, and the Army was looking for equipment for the Corps of Engineers and others which they did not have and sorely needed. The first demand was for the Navy.

John T. Mason, Jr.: You responded very readily, I take it, to the request to come down.

Admiral Moran: I went as promptly as I could—within a week.

John T. Mason, Jr.: This must have been inconvenient as far as your business was concerned; what was your position in the company then?

---

* Rear Admiral Emory S. Land, USN (Ret.), served as chairman of the U.S. Maritime Commission from February 1938 to January 1946. See his book *Winning the War with Ships* (New York: R. M. McBride Co., 1958).

Admiral Moran: I was then chairman of the company, and my place was taken by my uncle.

John T. Mason, Jr.: The same uncle who had been so prominent in World War I?

Admiral Moran: That's right. And my cousin, who was really in charge of operations here.

The requisition for equipment was dealt with by the Maritime Commission under the Merchant Marine Act of 1936, and it was with considerable difficulty that a major phase of the act was dealt with, because it provided that the vessels taken and the value of them was not to be enhanced by the causes necessitating the taking. That was in Section IX of the act.

John T. Mason, Jr.: Does that mean when it came time to return it that it would be the same price that they could get then?

Admiral Moran: It did not mean that, because the vessel was taken either for charter or for title, and in the main at the outset the vessels were taken for title. It simply meant that as a result of the war in Europe, the demand in the United States and elsewhere had caused substantial enhancement in the value of the vessel. The Congress required that this enhancement be disregarded, and the owner whose vessel was requisitioned felt it was worth far more than the determination made of the craft by the Maritime Commission. The owner who would disagree with this determination that the Maritime Commission made could accept 25% of the value so determined and sue for the balance. It took considerable persuasion and considerable legal talent in the Maritime Commission to convince the owner of the justice of the act. But there were some who sued and in the main were disappointed when the courts agreed with the Maritime Administration's interpretation of the act.

John T. Mason, Jr.: You say some, Admiral. Roughly how many took it into the court?

Admiral Moran: I would suppose that maybe a dozen out of 500 or 600.

John T. Mason, Jr.: But the persuading them not to do so, to accept the evaluation of the administration, this was largely your task, was it?

Admiral Moran: This was our task. I interviewed the greater proportion of the protesters. I am not sure that I convinced them of the righteousness of the determination, but I think that they reached the decision that they might as well accept their valuation and sue, although we certainly endeavored to litigate if they thought we were wrong. We had professional appraisers advising us, professionals in the field of yachts and small ships, tugs, barges, and all sorts of small craft. The British took about ten very good tugs, which they badly needed, and kept them until the end of the war, when they offered them back to the Maritime Commission. But they were valueless from that point of view at that particular time.

John T. Mason, Jr.: They were worn out, I take it.

Admiral Moran: They were not only worn out, but they were at distant places over the world, and they were changed to suit the accommodations of the foreign seamen.

John T. Mason, Jr.: You said small vessels—what tonnage were they largely?

Admiral Moran: The smallest vessel that we sent was of about 150 tons; the largest vessel we sent was about 350 tons.

John T. Mason, Jr.: That was to the British?

Admiral Moran: That was to the British.

John T. Mason, Jr.: How were they transported over there?

Admiral Moran: They went over under their own power.

John T. Mason, Jr.: In convoy?

Admiral Moran: No, I think they went over separately. I'm not sure about that. The British undertook that. They accepted them here and delivered them themselves.

John T. Mason, Jr.: And they lost none en route?

Admiral Moran: None that I know of. After the British had been dealt with and when war was declared, I continued, and the demands were much greater after Pearl Harbor.

John T. Mason, Jr.: I suppose Pearl Harbor made a difference with the owners, too, did it?

Admiral Moran: Pearl Harbor made a difference with everyone.

John T. Mason, Jr.: Prior to Pearl Harbor, when you had to present some arguments to the owners in order to get these craft, do you remember what sort of argument you presented?

Admiral Moran: Then their position was somewhat different in that they had much business, and they felt that their equipment was performing a more useful service than that which we were proposing to requisition it for.

John T. Mason, Jr.: In part there was truth in that, wasn't there?

Admiral Moran: There was substantial truth in that, but the greater value was in active war duty. We sent equipment to Greenland; we sent equipment to the South Pacific, the Southwest Pacific, and to Europe.

John T. Mason, Jr.: This was setting up bases, wasn't it?

Admiral Moran: Setting up bases and towing barges to these areas, towing equipment, different kinds of equipment that were needed in the port areas.

John T. Mason, Jr.: Were the Seabees in operation at that point?*

Admiral Moran: Yes, they just commenced.

John T. Mason, Jr.: So you must have worked with them?

Admiral Moran: Yes, to a degree we worked with them. Our instructions came through the Chief of Naval Operations' office: "We need this," and the Maritime Commission was charged with finding the needed equipment. I was in charge of developing a staff who could not only find the equipment but inspect it and determine its condition for more or less arduous service and lack of proper maintenance of these bases. There weren't facilities for carrying on proper maintenance.

John T. Mason, Jr.: Did you have any direct relationship with Admiral Ben Morrell?†

Admiral Moran: I did once or twice, yes, but he sent his requests through the office of the Chief of Naval Operations.

There was a wholesale demand for all kinds of equipment, and we requisitioned it and sent it out to them. It is interesting—when the Navy sought equipment, particularly for port use and piloting on the coast—when they inspected the vessel, they made a determination for their own information as to its value, and that determination became known to the owner of the vessel, who regarded it as final. But it wasn't final; it was our

---

* Seabees is the nickname applied to members of the Navy's mobile construction battalions (CBs).
† In 1937 Rear Admiral Ben Moreell, CEC, USN, became Chief of the Bureau of Yards and Docks. He held the position until 1945, after World War II had ended, having been promoted to vice admiral in 1944. He was in charge of developing the wartime naval shore establishment, which amounted to some 900 installations around the world.

determination, and our determination was vastly different than the inexperienced naval officer's. He was a great naval officer, competent in every way, but his competency didn't extend to determining the value of a yacht, or a tug, or a barge.

John T. Mason, Jr.: Did he overvalue?

Admiral Moran: He overvalued, and part of our difficulty was in persuading the owner that this valuation was invalid; it wasn't in prescription of the law, and it wasn't actual.

John T. Mason, Jr.: That was difficult, wasn't it, because they accepted the word of the Navy?

Admiral Moran: That was very difficult; they accepted the word of the Navy and thought it was as good as their bond.

John T. Mason, Jr.: I would think, as you got involved in this, that it would have been well not to have the Navy give an evaluation.

Admiral Moran: We tried to persuade them not to, but in their efforts to appease the owner who was going to lose his vessel, they inquired of him as to what he thought it was worth, and more often than not they accepted his word as to its value, which wasn't at all what the market was, nor was it a figure that was not enhanced by the causes necessitating its taking. That is precisely the way the act read, and we had a gathering of three judges of the Circuit Court of Appeals come to Washington and listen to the manner we used to make this determination of just compensation.

John T. Mason, Jr.: An educational course for the justices.

Admiral Moran: Yes, I think one judge was Hutchinson, and he was very able. They decided, I'm sure, that we were acting well within the Constitution.

A great problem we had was with the sardine fishermen out on the West Coast. Their fleet was not usable at all; it was laid up for the most part because of enemy action, and they couldn't agree at all with the idea of no enhancement. The vessels were laid up; they were out of commission; they were losing money by the day, and they thought, "Here is our opportunity to get rid of these boats at what it would cost to replace them." Because they thought surely they would be gone, and while we tried to work out a replacement, to devaluate it or depreciate it in value for the years that they had been in service, so they would have a new boat—depreciated. But that wouldn't go.

John T. Mason, Jr.: What were those boats destined for?

Admiral Moran: They would do patrol; they would go offshore.

John T. Mason, Jr.: How big were they?

Admiral Moran: They were 75 or 80 feet; they were good sea boats. They could go offshore and protect the port entrances. Half the time we didn't know what they wanted to do with them; we just knew that they wanted them. Admiral Land, and the Maritime Commission, really, delegated their power to the division that I was in and representing them in the requisitioning of the equipment.

John T. Mason, Jr.: He had a great deal of confidence in you? Had you known him before?

Admiral Moran: I went to see him once before, and he threw me out of his office. I went to see him about getting some help to build some equipment, and he said, "No, we're not bothering with that. Good day." But we got to know each other, and when I thought he was in error, I suggested that he change the view that he held. I think he admired that characteristic. He gained confidence, because we were really saving the government an enormous amount of money, and that was discovered by the complaints which were going to him. We had complaints from many prominent people. Mrs. Roosevelt was the recipient of a substantial number of letters complaining about the decrease in the value of the yacht that her friend owned or that she had recommended.* I will say this for her: she never suggested that we change our views; she merely brought the complaint to our attention and asked for an explanation, the reasoning back of it.

John T. Mason, Jr.: You came to that job with tremendous assets. Your contacts through your business must have been very helpful.

Admiral Moran: I was more helpful with commercial vessels; I really knew that market. There weren't as many complaints. I guess some competitors thought that I wasn't doing justice to them for a variety of reasons, but I never consciously changed a price for any ulterior motive.

John T. Mason, Jr.: You always, from your manhood on, had a reputation for great integrity. This was known about the field, wasn't it?

Admiral Moran: I think it was generally felt that way.

John T. Mason, Jr.: About the yachts in particular—a number of patriotic people turned their yachts in willingly with Pearl Harbor, did they not?

Admiral Moran: Yes, but they changed to a degree. When the war was over, they either didn't want the yacht back, or they wanted it back in the same condition it was in when it was turned over, which was not an unreasonable request. Some owners felt that, regardless of the cost, they ought to have the vessel restored, and we had some problems too. We had calls from the White House. These were people well known to the White House or well known to the secretaries. I would have a call from one of the President's secretaries asking if I had some free time during the day, and could I see this person or that. And I would always agree to see the fellow.

---

* Eleanor Roosevelt was the wife of President Franklin D. Roosevelt.

Congressman Schuyler Otis Bland made frequent inquiries, and one of my assistants, he said, had been discourteous, rebuffed one of his constituents, so I took the blame for that, unconsciously or unknowingly.* I spoke to Congressman Bland, and Admiral Land spoke to Congressman Bland. And he wrote a letter back and said no, it was not I—that I had done nothing but courteously treated all his constituents. Admiral Land had trouble, too, with some people who wrote to him and complained.

I think what we saved the government in decreasing the valuations which either the owner had requested or the Navy had suggested—we saved on a smallish number about $12 million. These vessels were not in the highest range. I spoke to Mr. Dupont, who had a yacht called the *Marmot*. He called to say he thought the value was low, and he would like to talk to me, so I said, "Certainly, I will be glad to talk with you."

"Well," he said, "do you want me to come over to Washington?"

I said, "No. You frequently go to New York, don't you? Why don't we meet on the train? I go up once a week sometimes, and we could arrange to meet on the train and discuss it. I think we are right."

He said, "Okay, I'll let you know." Then he called back, and he said, "Forget it. We'll take [your evaluation]."

Harold Vanderbilt had a yacht, *Bara*, and we requisitioned it.† It was in an unfinished state, and we determined $300,000. So he said, "Do you ever come to New York? I don't like to go down to Washington."

I said, "Yes, I do."

And he said, "Let me know when you are coming to New York; give me a ring." So, in due course, I gave him a ring, and I met with him at a club over there—downtown. We sat down, and he said, "What do you think that thing is worth?"

And I said, "We determined $300,000."

And he said, "That's all right; I'll take it." So we finished lunch, and when he got

---

* Schuyler Otis Bland, a Democrat from Virginia, served in the House of Representatives from 2 July 1918 until his death at the naval hospital, Bethesda, Maryland, 16 February 1950. The cargo ship *Schuyler Otis Bland* was named in his honor and later served with the Navy's Military Sea Transportation Service.
† Harold Sterling Vanderbilt (1884-1970) was the last of the famous Vanderbilt Family to direct the New York Central Railroad.

the check he signed it over to the USO.* He just endorsed the check over, the whole thing, which was very fitting.

John T. Mason, Jr.: What was the evaluation placed on the famed *Nourmahal*?

Admiral Moran: The *Nourmahal* was given to the service for one dollar, and later Vincent Astor thought that he ought to give the title to the vessel to the service, and there was a good deal of talk about it. I really don't know how it wound up, except he was compensated for the vessel.† It was after I left, and the Navy sold it to a Texan, and it was hauled down to somewhere in the gulf, where it took fire and was determined to be a total loss. I served with Vincent Astor on the Eastern Sea Frontier and got to know him very well.

Colonel Davies's wife owned a yacht called the *Sea Cloud*.‡ He was ambassador to Russia at the time, and he was very disappointed at the whole procedure, the determination of just compensation. I suspect it was taken out of our hands, because he really used all the influence he could gather.

John T. Mason, Jr.: He had a certain amount of political clout.

Admiral Moran: He did, oh yes, he did. He used it.

John T. Mason, Jr.: A number of people turned over smaller yachts—not these big, pretentious ones—and made arrangements to go with the yacht and offered their own personal services, and they became reserves in the Coast Guard. Did this help in any way?

---

* USO—United Services Organization is a group of U.S. civilians who put on entertainment programs for service personnel and provide hospitality for them in many parts of the world.
† The 2,250-ton, 215-foot-long yacht *Nourmahal* was acquired by the Navy from William Vincent Astor by a bareboat charter agreement on 3 March 1942, to be operated by a Coast Guard crew. She was given the Navy hull number PG-72. On 29 June 1943 she was purchased by the Navy for $300,000 under an option in the original charter agreement. She was transferred to the Coast Guard 29 December 1943 and designated with the new hull number WPG-72 and served until decommissioned 30May 1946.
‡ Joseph E. Davies served as U.S. Ambassador to the Soviet Union from 25 January 1937 to 11 June 1938.

Admiral Moran: We didn't get those things; they weren't requisitioned. They were just in use by the Coast Guard and subject to Coast Guard instructions. We didn't get them, because the owner stayed with them and acted as owner representing the Coast Guard. That died out; it was a futility. It didn't function well enough. The yachts were too small.

John T. Mason, Jr.: It seemed to me that it was perhaps a flush of enthusiasm at the outset of the war.

Admiral Moran: Oh, sure, sure, sure.

John T. Mason, Jr.: The Coast Guard also was charged very shortly with the protection of harbors, and this required a lot of small vessels, did it not? Were they a part of the requisitioning effort?

Admiral Moran: Well, some of them may have been, but we didn't get many from the Coast Guard; the Coast Guard seemed to immune themselves. We had very few Coast Guard titles or charters.

John T. Mason, Jr.: Of course, they became part of the Navy with Pearl Harbor and even before Pearl Harbor.[*]

Admiral Moran: That's right; that's right. War was declared in December, and I was in the Maritime Commission. The Maritime Commission was running ships on the coast, and the submarines came over, and the ships were getting torpedoed. The hope was that vessels could be rescued and salvaged. But there was no organization in position to do the rescue phase of salvage.

John T. Mason, Jr.: So I see another job coming up for you.

---

[*] As authorized by Congress, President Roosevelt on 1 November 1941 ordered the Coast Guard to "operate as part of the Navy, subject to the orders of the Secretary of the Navy." The Coast Guard returned to the Treasury Department on 1 January 1946.

Admiral Moran: I was enrolled in the Naval Reserve as a lieutenant commander.

John T. Mason, Jr.: At this point, if I may read into the tape, I would like to, a paragraph from Admiral Land's letter of November 5, 1943 to Admiral Jacobs, who was in charge of personnel in the Navy.[*] It was in connection with your commission, and he spoke about your work in the Maritime Administration. He said you had:

> ". . . been charged with procurement of all conventional vessels of a thousand tons and under, for the Navy and War Department. He determines the valuation and charter rates and negotiations in settlement of claims of the owners. More than 2,500 vessels have been acquired and appraised in this fashion."

That was one paragraph in his letter which I took from your files, and I thought I'd read that onto the record at this point.

All right, sir, this other job was coming up as a result of the war.

Admiral Moran: The Navy had a contract with Merritt-Chapman, and Scott for salvaging vessels stranded or in danger of sinking and becoming a total loss. This was a World War contract which continued during enemy action on the coast. Merritt-Chapman were thoroughly capable of going out and towing the vessel in, but the same vessel which was capable of towing the damaged vessel in the salvage operation—getting it pumped out, pulled off the beach, or whatever. Captain Davis, who was vice president—I was a great friend of his; we had known each other for some time—I used to lunch with him frequently, and we would talk openly.[†] He was considerably older than I was, and he was a man who regarded honor as the greatest of virtues. He told me that he thought he never told a lie, except on one occasion when he lied about the number of bags of sugar in a draft that was being loaded on a vessel of which he was captain.

John T. Mason, Jr.: That must have been reminiscent in your mind of your stepfather.

---

[*] Rear Admiral Randall Jacobs, USN, served as Chief of the Bureau of Navigation/Personnel from 19 December 1941 to 15 September 1945. He was promoted to vice admiral as of 1 February 1944.
[†] Captain Walter N. Davis.

Admiral Moran: Yes, it was. He was really a great man, resourceful, truthful, modest, and energetic, willing to try. He never trimmed his sails to agree with anyone with whom he couldn't agree. He was really a great person. He taught me a lot, and I listened to him carefully and tried to exemplify his courage and disposition.

John T. Mason, Jr.: He had a great reputation in this area, did he not, in New York, and great influence?

Admiral Moran: All through the United States. He had done wonderful jobs; he took jobs that looked impossible to do. Anyhow, he suggested to the Navy that they appoint an officer whose duty would be to gather equipment that could go out on the coast and rescue a vessel that had been broken down but was still afloat, bring her on the beach or, if possible, to the nearest safe port. The Assistant Chief of the Bureau of Ships, who was then, I think, Admiral Earle Mills, talked it over, and it was agreed between Mills and Admiral Land that I ought to organize this thing.[*]

John T. Mason, Jr.: Did Captain Davis urge this in any way?

Admiral Moran: He urged that we do the thing, so I requisitioned, I guess, seven or eight big, powerful tugs to stand by Miami and New York and pick up the convoys coming out of the Gulf of Mexico bound up here—mainly petroleum cargoes, tankers.

John T. Mason, Jr.: And prime targets of the German submarines.

Admiral Moran: They were ripping them off by the dozen. They were hitting cargo ships—carrying bulk commodities, lumber, sugar. The fleet was organized.

John T. Mason, Jr.: And what was this time?

---

[*] Rear Admiral Earle W. Mills, USN, served as Assistant Chief of the Bureau of Ships from November 1942 to November 1945.

Admiral Moran: This was, I think, May of 1942. What we would do was to put the tug in a convoy to proceed with it, maintain convoy speed if possible. Sometimes it was impossible; it was a little too rough for the tug to make the headway that the big ships made. Anyway, we stuck to it, and one day we received word that the *Manhattan*, a troopship, had taken fire off the coast of Nova Scotia.[*] The Admiral of the Eastern Sea Frontier, Adolphus Andrews, said, "This is our job."[†] I guess the Chief of Naval Operations had said to him, "Get that ship in."

John T. Mason, Jr.: Did it have troops on board?

Admiral Moran: No, it was coming back. It had some troops, I think, who were ill, but I'm not too certain about that. Admiral Andrews's chief of staff was Thomas Kurtz, a captain who had retired; he had been commandant of the Naval Academy.[‡] He came back and was on active duty at the Eastern Sea Frontier. He called me and said, ""We've got to get that ship in!" She was afire. The cruiser *Brooklyn* had taken most of the crew off and such soldiers as were returning, but she wouldn't stand by the ship. There were destroyers out there, but they had to keep pretty far away because they were being silhouetted by the fire. I got on the job and sent, I think, four of our rescue tugs out to get it.

John T. Mason, Jr.: These were Navy tugs or your own?

Admiral Moran: This was the rescue fleet. It didn't comprise any of Moran's tugs at all. Commander Eastern Sea Frontier called the Navy, I think. They had a base up there somewhere.

John T. Mason, Jr.: Casco Bay they were.

---

[*] USS *Wakefield* (AP-21) was formerly the passenger ship *Manhattan* of the United States Lines. On 3 September 1942 while bound for New York during a transatlantic convoy crossing, she caught fire and was abandoned. The light cruiser *Brooklyn* (CL-40) rescued 1,173 troops from the transport. Although she was severely damaged by the fire, the *Wakefield* was towed to safety and repaired.

[†] Vice Admiral Adolphus Andrews, USN.

[‡] Captain Thomas R. Kurtz, USN, served as the Naval Academy's commandant of midshipmen from 1921 to 1924. He retired from active duty in 1929 and then was recalled for World War II service.

Admiral Moran: And they had tugs up there, but they wouldn't let them out. They couldn't spare them, which I thought was unbelievable.

John T. Mason, Jr.: They were near at hand.

Admiral Moran: And here's a valuable troopship. So we sent the civilian tugs out, and they got the ship and brought her into Halifax. I sent a man from here, a civilian in this office, Captain Earl Palmer, out to the ship. He went aboard the ship and helped the captain in the management and communication with the tugs, because they were civilian tugs. They had no idea of naval communication.

We brought the ship into Halifax, and then we brought her down to the Boston Navy Yard. Everybody thought it was a great job—wartime—pulled her along about five knots; she was terribly damaged. I went up to Boston to see that there was no difficulty in getting her in and putting her in the dock. The only thing different about it was that it was wartime, and there were submarines out there. But we had two destroyers; they stayed way off and were ready to help in case they were needed. The captain of the ship was in pretty bad shape; the vessel was almost gutted. We got her in.

That gave the civilian rescue service, operated by the Navy, paid for the Maritime Commission, a combination that was hard to believe. The vessels were managed by civilian operators, the people who owned them. This was the queerest kind of thing you ever knew, but it worked. We lost one tug. We lost the *John R. Williams*, which was owned by the Great Lakes Dredge and Dock Company; she struck a mine at the entrance of the Delaware and was blown to pieces. The captain, Roy Allen, was lost; the chief engineer was lost, and some others were lost. It was sad.

John T. Mason, Jr.: That was one of our own mines, wasn't it?

Admiral Moran: Oh, yes, I guess so. I think it was, but we had been pretty fairly informed as to the location of the mines. The German submarines were out there laying mines, and I don't know whether it was one of theirs or ours. But, in any case, we did the job.

John T. Mason, Jr.: Now, you were in uniform by this time, weren't you?

Admiral Moran: Oh yes, I was a lieutenant commander. I got a promotion out of Washington.

John T. Mason, Jr.: Tell me about getting into uniform, because you had a little problem, didn't you, in that you were too much underweight or something?

Admiral Moran: I was too much underweight, but they smoked it out for me fairly well. I had a heart murmur too. The doctor picked that up right away, but they waived everything. I think I weighed about 110 pounds; I was very light. I got up to 117 by a forced diet.

John T. Mason, Jr.: And then they let you in, so you were a man of authority.

Admiral Moran: Yes. By that time, the thing was pretty well managed. That went into 1942—the rescue aspect.

John T. Mason, Jr.: Before you say that, I want to refer again to your getting commissioned as lieutenant commander and all the letters of commendation in your file, all dated in March of 1942. There's one by Huntington T. Morse, as chairman of the Maritime Commission; James H. Ward, vice president of Bethlehem Steel; W. N. Davis, vice president of Merritt-Chapman, Scott; and Captain J. T. Stapler—all of them nice letters. I suppose all that helped, but you were destined for that job anyway. And in September 1942 you got promoted to commander.

Admiral Moran: Yes, that was after the war started. What did they say about that?

John T. Mason, Jr.: Well, Jerry Land wrote a letter to Admiral Jacobs supporting your elevation to commander, and in his own handwriting he wrote, "I am particularly keen on this promotion, thoroughly deserved. Jerry Land." There was also one from Adolphus Andrews.

What other ventures were you involved in during this time you were serving with the Navy?

Admiral Moran: When it became certain to the Maritime Commission that there would be an insufficiency of self-propelled cargo ships of 10,000 tons deadweight, the suggestion was made to them that the construction of concrete barges could supplant or take the place of the ships which couldn't be built in quantities sufficient to meet the needs of the prospective overseas trades.[*] There was a very considerable doubt as to the suitability of concrete barges. Their seaworthiness was questioned; their stability was questioned; and their rigidity was questioned. They would draw too much water.

John T. Mason, Jr.: These questions arose in the Bureau of Ships?

Admiral Moran: In the Bureau of Ships and in the Maritime Commission. So a hearing was held; I was invited to the hearing.

John T. Mason, Jr.: Now, this was approximately when?

Admiral Moran: This was at the early days of the conflict, early in 1942. Those invited were shippers, constructors, labor representatives, shipbuilders, and experts in concrete construction. I was invited to discuss feasibility of towing these barges should they be built. Everyone agreed that the concrete barge could meet a requirement. They were not to be self-propelled; they were to be towed.

John T. Mason, Jr.: How heavy were they to be?

---

[*] Deadweight is the term for a ship's load, including the total weight of cargo, fuel, stores, crew, and passengers. It is generally used to refer to commercial ships rather than naval vessels.

Admiral Moran: They were to have a capacity of about 9,000 tons. The program was adopted, and the concrete barges were to be built mainly in the South in shipyards which were then available or ship-repair yards which could be fitted to build vessels. They weren't to be built in any of the big standard yards, because there would be a conflict.

John T. Mason, Jr.: Was this entirely an innovative idea? Had there been concrete barges before?

Admiral Moran: Yes. Some years ago there had been. So the concrete barge construction plan was adopted, and contracts were let.

John T. Mason, Jr.: What number was anticipated?

Admiral Moran: I really have forgotten, but there were 50 tugs contracted for to tow these barges. These were oceangoing tugs.

John T. Mason, Jr.: What shipbuilder was largely concerned about building tugs?

Admiral Moran: Well, there were shipbuilders in New England, on the Great Lakes, in the South, on the West Coast. These were tugs about 200 feet long, 2,500 shaft horsepower, diesel.

John T. Mason, Jr.: That was quite considerable horsepower, wasn't it?

Admiral Moran: It was in those days, yes. And they had good range, fair endurance, large capacity for fuel.

John T. Mason, Jr.: Long legged you called them.

Admiral Moran: Yes. So the tugs were finished, and the barges weren't. The first of the tugs came along at the beginning of 1943, I should say. And there were no barges, but there was plenty of work for tugs to do, and here they were. So the Maritime Commission decided that they would operate them, and they would appoint an operator. Well, there were very few operators—substantially no operators on this coast who operated large seagoing tugs, except this company.

John T. Mason, Jr.: Except Moran Towing.

Admiral Moran: So it was decided by the Maritime Commission that the tugs would be operated by Moran, and then there was the question of my being in Washington.

John T. Mason, Jr.: Conflict of interest?

Admiral Moran: Yes, conflict, but nobody seemed to care. Nobody wanted the darn things, because they didn't have the personnel for them, and they weren't aware of what the magnitude of the business was going to be. So there were no complaints about Moran getting these tugs. We took them here. The company manned them, operated them, repaired them, got them fuel, got them crews, and stood by on orders from Maritime. The Navy would give the orders to Maritime, and Maritime would do it. When some areas of the Navy realized what a potential they had here, they sought to have them transferred to the Navy from the Maritime, but the Chief of Naval Personnel and Earle Mills decided that they oughtn't to be Navy manned. They ought to be manned by civilians, because they carried a crew of 36, including a gun crew.

John T. Mason, Jr.: They had to be armed?

Admiral Moran: If they were taken into the Navy, they probably would have taken 100 in the crew; they hadn't the accommodations for 100. They would have had to be torn apart and a fortune spent to man them the way the Navy managed a similar type called the ATA, which had about like power but half the fuel capacity. They had big forecastles, and these vessels did not need any forecastle at all. They would run as civilians, with probably 20 crew; the Navy was still running with 100.

The first thing that happened was there was a shortage of lubricating oil in Nouméa, where there was a base.* We requisitioned three Mississippi River barges, loaded them with lubricating oils in New Orleans, and we took them from New Orleans to Nouméa, towed them 9,000 miles.

John T. Mason, Jr.: Through the Panama Canal?

Admiral Moran: Through the Panama Canal. Thereafter, we did all kinds of jobs with those ATAs. We used them at Normandy; we towed dry docks to the South Pacific; we rescued Navy ships in the South Pacific; we towed to Bermuda; we did everything. I have the list of miles that we covered with the 50 tugs, and I'll give that to you. It's on my wall at home.

John T. Mason, Jr.: Were there any mishaps or anything of the sort in all that effort. Were they attacked by the enemy ever?

Admiral Moran: We lost one tug, a little one. When she was in tow, she broke away from the big tugs. The operation was phenomenal, really unbelievable. No one could fully comprehend it. We had six or seven of them in Normandy.

John T. Mason, Jr.: Were they under your direction?

Admiral Moran: They were always under my direction in a sense.

John T. Mason, Jr.: Meanwhile, were you still requisitioning small vessels?

Admiral Moran: No, that was over. That was a failure, useless expense. They had sailboats out there on the coast, maybe to scare somebody away one time, I don't know.

---

* Nouméa, New Caledonia, in the South Pacific.

When we got this Navy equipment delivered where we wanted, I was in Washington. A young man came in the office one day and said he was sent there by the Chief of Naval Operations. He asked me questions, and it would be helpful if I could answer them.

John T. Mason, Jr.: He was sent there by Admiral King then?*

Admiral Moran: Yes, or King's office. He asked me a lot about ground tackle and beach operations, but he didn't tell me why he was asking the questions.† He asked me about unloading on beaches. He was a naval officer, and I told him all I could.

John T. Mason, Jr.: You probably were guessing all the time.

Admiral Moran: I didn't know what this was. The next thing that happened, Admiral Stark sent for me; he was over there at the General Board of the Navy on Constitution Avenue.‡ He said, "I might like to have you come over and take a look at a plan that is being considered. You come to London and spend a few days. Give me your opinion of certain aspects of it and go home."

I said, "Of course, I will be glad to do that.

The next thing I knew, the Army called and asked for a type of unit that could get up on the beach and be discharged when the tide was low.

John T. Mason, Jr.: You mean an LST?§

Admiral Moran: This was not to be an LST; this they thought ought to be a barge, so I kind of thought of the thing and decided that a railroad car float would be the right unit for the purpose.

---

* Admiral Ernest J. King, USN, served as Chief of Naval Operations from 26 March 1942 to 15 December 1945; he was promoted to the rank of fleet admiral in December 1944.
† Ground tackle is a general term for all the anchoring equipment on board a ship.
‡ Admiral Harold R. Stark, USN, served as Commander U.S. Naval Forces Europe from 30 April 1942 to 15 August 1945.
§ LST—tank landing ship, an amphibious warfare ship capable of putting her bow directly onto a beach, opening bow doors, and lowering a bow ramp to permit vehicles to exit.

John T. Mason, Jr.: Why did you think of the railroad car float?

Admiral Moran: Because it was very long, and it had very low sides, short sides. It wasn't a deep vessel at all; it would run up to 220 feet long, and it would have maybe 7- or 8-foot sides. It had no longitudinal strength. That was the disadvantage. But it could go on the beach, and when the tide would drop 10 feet, as it would, the barge was high and dry, and they could just take the stuff off with ramps easily.

John T. Mason, Jr.: Was this before the LST had come into existence?

Admiral Moran: No, the LST was being built, but it was a personnel carrier for the main part, or a tank carrier, or a vehicle carrier. The small landing craft for personnel, the LCI, was too small for this proposition. This proposition was to carry 10,000 tons of K rations, gasoline, and ammunition.[*] That's a fairly substantial load.

John T. Mason, Jr.: When was that revealed to you—the fact that that was the requirement? It was not at the beginning?

Admiral Moran: I cannot tell you precisely when, but it was not at the outset. So the problem was to requisition the equipment. The general in the Army was the fellow who did the WPA.[†] We went to the railroads, all of the railroads in New York, and asked them if they could spare a car float.

John T. Mason, Jr.: How many were you seeking?

Admiral Moran: Twelve. And they said no, they couldn't.

---

[*] The K ration was a U.S. Army field ration used in World War II. A day's ration contained three small cardboard boxes, each enough for one meal.
[†] WPA—Works Progress Administration, a Depression-relief agency that sometimes created make-work projects in order to stimulate employment.

John T. Mason, Jr.: They were so overburdened.

Admiral Moran: Then we explained the need for them, and while they were very sympathetic they said, "We simply won't be able to do the job if you take that number of floats from us." So we decided we would take some oil barges that had some comparative dimensions. They were flat, they were a little deeper, and they had better sides so that they were more immune to the dangers of breaking in half on the way over to France. Anyway, we took a lot of equipment.

John T. Mason, Jr.: Did the oil people holler?

Admiral Moran: Yes, everyone hollered, but nobody was aware, or no one could comprehend a need greater than theirs.

John T. Mason, Jr.: That's human, isn't it?

Admiral Moran: Yes, but we took the car floats.

John T. Mason, Jr.: There was no possibility of having them manufactured?

Admiral Moran: No, not then, because this was late in 1943, and we felt we had to get away—I asked for a date that we could depart here. I didn't need to know the date they were going to invade France, but I asked for a date to depart here.

John T. Mason, Jr.: Meanwhile, had Stark carried out his thought that you would have to go to London and see plans? Did you do that?

Admiral Moran: That was in it, sure. He thought I was going there to look over the thing and see if it was well organized and the American Army was being properly protected and so on. So we requisitioned the floats, and then the question was how to get those darn things over.

I called up a friend of mine, Captain George S. Bull. He was chief surveyor for the United States Salvage Association. The U.S. Salvage Association is an organization that's owned and operated by the American Underwriters, and it's the inspection agency for them, the surveying agency for them. They determine the damage that they are obliged to assume on behalf of the underwriters to repair, to estimate its costs, and to estimate the suitability of a ship for insurance—inspectors, as it were, and very skillful people they are and were.

So we had a meeting, and it was decided that the only way we could get these car floats over to England was to put one of them on a dry dock—lift it out of the water—and take a plate or two off its bottom, then sink the dry dock so that the car float became immersed and filled with water. Then put a new car float on top of the bottom float, then raise the dry dock, drain the water out of the bottom of the car float, weld the two of them together, and you have one unit with double the longitudinal strength of the single car float, strap them together by electric welding, close the car float's bottom up, drop it again, and float the two of them off.

John T. Mason, Jr.: What would something like that weigh—two car floats, one on top of the other.

Admiral Moran: Well, I suppose they would weigh about the amount of the steel that was in them, and I would venture there would be about 400 tons of steel, maybe 500, but it was nothing. Each one had a capacity to lift 1,000 tons.

John T. Mason, Jr.: What an ingenious idea; how did you arrive at that?

Admiral Moran: We discussed the problem, but the main man was Captain George Bull. He supervised it; he took it over; he did it. We got those car floats fixed; we got, I think, eight oil barges; and we started a convoy. I don't think we lost anything. We may have lost one unit; I've really forgotten. We used all civilian tugs except a few Navy. This was in the springtime. I think we left April 21 or 22.

John T. Mason, Jr.: And the speed of such a convoy?

Admiral Moran: It would run along about six knots, a slow convoy. A tanker went with them to keep them supplied with fuel oil. Some were steamers, and some were diesel generated. They landed in Normandy.

John T. Mason, Jr.: It must have been an object of some speculation to the German submariners to see a convoy of this sort.

Admiral Moran: I guess it was. We only lost one tug, and that tug was running free. She was going around collecting the mail, and she ran into one of the tugs and sank. That was the only loss we had. There was a further loss. They tried it again, and I'll get to this soon.

John T. Mason, Jr.: Where did you take them in April?

Admiral Moran: We took them to Cardiff, where the barges were dismantled and put afloat on their own bottoms and brought to Plymouth, where they were loaded with ammunition, K rations, and gasoline. That was eventually. Because they got there around the 24th or 25th of May; it took them a month to get across and to their loading berth. I saw them in Plymouth and inspected them. I should think it was the 15th or 20th of May. On June 6 we took them across the channel, and they were a lifesaver.

John T. Mason, Jr.: They delivered what the Army required?

Admiral Moran: They delivered what the Army required.

John T. Mason, Jr.: In that connection, Admiral, there is a story which Admiral Jimmy Hall told me, and also Admiral Kirk told me, about the argument that General Bradley had with Hall on Omaha Beach about the delivery of ammunition.[*] He was demanding that it be done, and he was trying to put the blame on Hall for not having it there. Hall said it was the Army's task to get it there. Do you recall the circumstances of that?

Admiral Moran: All I know is that it was told to me that General Bradley had made it a condition of his landing this Army group on the beaches that there would be the 10,000 tons of gasoline, K rations, and ammunition. And, to the best of my knowledge, we put it there. I never heard any controversy. It was there; what wasn't there wasn't put there by the craft that they thought could put it there, and that was some kind of landing craft. I know sometimes it wasn't there, because at times it didn't come fast enough.

John T. Mason, Jr.: I think that was a factor—it didn't come as fast as Bradley wanted it.

Admiral Moran: Yes, because General Ross, the Army transportation boss, sent a telegram to somebody, complaining about getting the stuff over, but I never comprehended the difficulties he was having. I went over there with General Eisenhower, and he was really very happy about what had been accomplished by these barges, and he thought it was an ingenious idea.[†] He thought it had saved the day. He thought so to such an extent that he got General Franklin over, and with him they decided that they wanted more of that equipment over there, and they spoke to me about it. General Eisenhower sent that telegram you saw to General Marshall and Admiral King, where he wanted another convoy. Now, this was about the 23rd or 24th of June.[‡]

John T. Mason, Jr.: This was after the storm.[§]

---

[*] Rear Admiral John L. Hall, USN, Commander XI Amphibious Force; Rear Admiral Alan G. Kirk, USN, Commander Western Naval Task Force; Lieutenant General Omar N. Bradley, USA, Commander First U.S. Army. Recollections from Admiral Hall and Admiral Kirk concerning the invasion of Normandy are contained in oral histories they did as part of the Columbia University program.
[†] General Dwight D. Eisenhower, USA, Supreme Allied Commander in Europe.
[‡] General George C. Marshall, USA, was the U.S. Army Chief of Staff.
[§] On 19 June 1944 the Normandy coast was hit by the longest English Channel storm during that season for many years. It lasted three days and caused heavy damage to the artificial harbors set up on the Normandy landing beaches.

Admiral Moran: After the storm, and I thought that there wasn't the equipment available, so they decided that they would ask the Maritime Commission to contract for ten more car floats.

John T. Mason, Jr.: You mean build them?

Admiral Moran: Yes, at the Sun yard in Chester, Pennsylvania.

John T. Mason, Jr.: There was a time factor there, wasn't there?

Admiral Moran: Yes, this was June, and we didn't get them ready until October. They left in October, and the thing was one of the greatest calamities there ever was. The fellow who wrote—I forget what it was called. It was a sheer disaster. They lost tugs; they lost barges en route.

John T. Mason, Jr.: Where were they to take them at that point?

Admiral Moran: They were gong to take them to Cardiff, I think. They were going to take them to a British port, I think. I never heard a thing about it, although he quotes me as having said that we ought to have another tug—just a free tug that would go picking these things up. Because, God knows, I know what October in the North Atlantic is.

John T. Mason, Jr.: You were back here by then?

Admiral Moran: Yes, I was back here. I never would have tried it.

John T. Mason, Jr.: Were they actually needed at that late date?

Admiral Moran: No.

John T. Mason, Jr.: By that time we had free access to the French ports, didn't we?

Admiral Moran: Sure. We had access to Cherbourg before I left there in August. It was a tremendous disaster, but they had the Army trying to do it with Navy escorts.

John T. Mason, Jr.: Why didn't they try to duplicate what had been done previously in April?

Admiral Moran: Nobody ever spoke about it, you know. It was a very difficult thing to do. I had no part of it. A cable came from Stark in October or November to Admiral Land. I was in Washington, and Stark asked for me to come over, but he wanted to know if I were willing. Land spoke to me and said, "Sure, if you want to go, go."

So I said, "Well, if he wants me, I'll go. But he never came through with it. But he overrated me a little bit. He thought I was a bright star.

John T. Mason, Jr.: You had produced in a moment of need, so naturally—

Admiral Moran: I came back after Normandy, and I went out to the Pacific.

John T. Mason, Jr.: But there are other things that you did at Normandy. Tell me when you went over there. You were only there for a month or two, weren't you?

Admiral Moran: I went over in April.

John T. Mason, Jr.: You went over in advance of the arrival of the convoy?

Admiral Moran: Oh, yes. I got there in April. I think I got there April 15.

John T. Mason, Jr.: What was your job when you got there?

Admiral Moran: When I got there, I didn't know what they wanted, really. They brought me to a great big room in which there were a lot of wall maps and simulations of the beach—houses and everything.

John T. Mason, Jr.: Was this in London?

Admiral Moran: Yes, and I had to sign the book.

John T. Mason, Jr.: This is the first time you knew to any extent the plans?

Admiral Moran: Yes, what they wanted and when. It looked like a reasonable thing to do, and I thought I could do it, but it was a great big mystery to them. They had a group of Navy people there. First of all, Stark sent me over to see if the thing was properly planned.

John T. Mason, Jr.: This was for the ammunition?

Admiral Moran: For the whole thing. I went down a place where there were a lot of British admirals and some American fellows. They told me what they had to do, and they told me what they thought the speeds would be, and they weren't far out. They were doing it in kind of an expensive way, but the problem was that they didn't have anybody on the far shore at Normandy that would handle these caissons in a comprehensive way and do it well.[*] I couldn't be in both places.

John T. Mason, Jr.: Now, you are talking about what came to be called the Mulberries, and you thought it was a reasonable idea that they had?

---

[*] Because the D-Day landings in France were made over open beaches rather than in a protected harbor, the Allies created artificial harbors by bringing from England a number of specially constructed concrete caissons nicknamed "Mulberries" that could be sunk offshore to form a breakwater and protect the unloading of cargo onto the beaches.

Admiral Moran: Yes, I thought it was reasonable to expect them to protect the beach by putting a harbor there. I went out with some of the people who were running some American tugs they had, and the fellows in the tugs were not competent to do this close work. And I couldn't stay there and work with them, because there were other things Admiral Stark had for me to do and the Army had to do and that the British had for me to do. So at a conference with the British, the man whom they had delegated to be the controller, a Britisher, went to his boss and said, "This guy can do this job better than I can do it. Let me out and put him in."

But the British officer said, "This is a British operation."

And they said, "We'll go see Admiral Stark and see what he says."

One officer said to the other, "We'd better not go see Admiral Stark; he's the commander of U.S. Naval Forces in Europe. We'd better go see Admiral Ramsay."[*] He was British and the senior naval commander of the operation. So they went to Stark, and Stark heard from Ramsay that they wanted me. Stark said I was to take the whole thing.

John T. Mason, Jr.: He didn't ask you?

Admiral Moran: He didn't ask me at all. He said, "You're going to do it." So I went down to a place where Admiral Ramsay was located, on the coast. I spoke to Admiral Ramsay, and he said he was going to ask me to relieve the captain who had been charged with being the controller of the operation.

John T. Mason, Jr.: Were you at that time a captain?

Admiral Moran: I was a captain. We had a hospital ship; we had a staff, we had WRNS for clerical people—a big operation.[†] So I said, "Okay."

John T. Mason, Jr.: At this point, will you give me the scope of the project?

---

[*] Admiral Sir Bertram Ramsay, RN, was Allied Naval Commander Expeditionary Force.
[†] WRNS—Women's Royal Naval Service. When pronounced, the acronym sounded like "wrens."

Admiral Moran: I'll do it. We had 90 caissons to tow.

John T. Mason, Jr.: And a caisson could be what?

Admiral Moran: The caisson was 200 feet long, 69 feet beam. It would contain, when loaded, 7,000 tons of weight, had a draft of about 23 feet.

John T. Mason, Jr.: There were 90 of these, and they were constructed of what?

Admiral Moran: They were constructed of reinforced concrete. We put them in a line. We put them with wings into the shore, and we also brought over pontoons upon which was fitted a pathway for vehicles—tanks and motorcars and a roadway for troops.

John T. Mason, Jr.: What was the time element? When were these to be towed and installed?

John T. Mason, Jr.: The first assault took place early morning on June 6.[*] We started across with the tows on the morning of June 6. The tows proceeded at the rate of five or six knots, and the distance was approximately 100 miles, coming from Portsmouth, Selsey, and Plymouth.

John T. Mason, Jr.: Was there any confusion because of the troops being transported?

Admiral Moran: No, there wasn't. There were pretty fair lanes established. The minefields were swept away, and the minesweepers were at the point of entrance to the beaches. The difficulty was to find the precise place where the caissons were to be dropped on the beach. They had ranges—houses on the beach, formation of the beach—where they could be sure that the pontoons were put in the right places. There were areas within the pontoons where vessels could go. The landing craft could go in to the beach.

---

[*] For an overall account of the operation, see Samuel Eliot Morison, *The Invasion of France and Germany, 1944-1945* (Boston: Little, Brown, 1957). Volume XI of History of United States Naval Operations in World War II. The book contains a description of the use of the Mulberries.

John T. Mason, Jr.: This required some very expert navigators on the tugs, did it not? Were they naval or civilian?

Admiral Moran: Oh, sure. They were civilians, and they were capable of doing it all right. And, of course, there were patrols there that would lead them in, because they were under constant fire from the shore batteries. The Navy ships were outside—the battleships were outside, firing and holding down some of the fire from shore. They blasted those shelters and the places where they were sure the Germans had their heaviest artillery. The people who suffered were the infantry that first day. They were right under the fire from the cliffs, and they had a terrible time getting up the cliff. They tried to get under, because they were shooting from both sides, and the beach was filled with impediments. They had railroad iron that was made in the form of a spike setting outward to prevent the landing craft landing. If a landing craft got on top of a spike, it was sufficient to puncture the landing craft. The weather was good, but it could have been better.

John T. Mason, Jr.: These cumbersome concrete caissons—that must have been a—

Admiral Moran: They were difficult to handle.

John T. Mason, Jr.: How many were being towed simultaneously?

Admiral Moran: Each of the tugs had one; of the big tugs I guess we must have had about 40 or 50. The rails were fitted like this and were bent like that. This one was the shorter length, and that was pointed up.

John T. Mason, Jr.: This is what the Germans did.

Admiral Moran: Yes, that's what the Germans did. And you'd come in with a barge, and if you'd get on top of it, it was sunk. You were holed.

John T. Mason, Jr.: If you had 40 or 50 tugs, you had approximately two jobs for each tug then? How long did it take to tow them over?

Admiral Moran: We could go over there in about 24 hours. We started on the seventh of June there. We brought a lot of railroad equipment over, too, bridge equipment, pontoon equipment. The pontoon consisted of something like this. This is a case pontoon, two circles, and they are watertight. This is the base of the bridge, and this is the bridge.

John T. Mason, Jr.: The bridges were really erected on pontoons. They were a bit top-heavy, weren't they?

Admiral Moran: No, and they'd float about here.

John T. Mason, Jr.: And that required what—about one tug?

Admiral Moran: No, these were 40 feet long—the bridges—and we had six of them, so we would have 480 feet of these things. And this required one tug, a small one. Some of the pontoons were like this—both the same size. This is looking at it broadside, and this looking at it head on. We loaded there until Cherbourg was captured.

John T. Mason, Jr.: There were two so-called harbors for this?

Admiral Moran: There were five beaches. The Americans had Omaha and Utah. The British had Gold, Sword, and Juno.

John T. Mason, Jr.: You were talking about the various beaches where these Mulberries had to be installed. Were the tugs attacked by air at any time during this time?

Admiral Moran: No, we had two tugs that were attacked by E-boats or a submarine.[*] I rather think it was an E-boat attack, but since one attacked at night it was not known by the crew of the tug who did it.

John T. Mason, Jr.: Was it sunk?

Admiral Moran: Yes, it was sunk. One Navy tug and one British tug, but there was no loss of life. The other tugs were under way and picked up the survivors. It was much less than we thought would happen.

John T. Mason, Jr.: Did you come under coastal gunfire?

Admiral Moran: They came under lots of fire on the Normandy coast, but none were hit because the planes were doing a pretty good job of protecting them and keeping them from surface craft. What they were doing from these embankments, they couldn't quite reach them.

John T. Mason, Jr.: The installation of the caissons to establish these artificial harbors, did it all work according to the plan that had been drawn up in Britain?

Admiral Moran: Yes, it all worked according to the plan; we brought the equipment over, all of it, and the British engineers and the American engineers had the job of locating them where they wanted them. But we supplied the tugs by which they did it. The tugs were under the experienced Captain Bassett. He was a very helpful man; he was the man I sent for and upon whom I relied for doing the job on the other side.

John T. Mason, Jr.: You knew his qualifications? Was he one of your men here?

---

[*] E-boat was the Allied designation for small, fast German motor torpedo boat, the equivalent of the U.S. PT boat.

Admiral Moran: He used to be, yes. He was very capable, and he was very courageous. He was a little bit bewildered by it all, because when he got over there he was up against more than he had anticipated.

John T. Mason, Jr.: Well, this was sort of a fantastic thing.

Admiral Moran: He stuck it out and did a very, very good job.

John T. Mason, Jr.: It brings up a question that you might discuss, if you will, and that is the practicality of the whole thing. There are those who maintain that they were sort of a British fantasy and not very useful. There were others thought they were extremely valuable, and you were one who thought so?

Admiral Moran: I don't think the assault on France could have been accomplished without it. I don't think there was a possibility of going on the open beaches without the protection that these harbors afforded. I don't think it could have been completed in half the time that it took for the whole adventure to be completed if you hadn't done it that way. It would have taken at least twice as long. These troops were going ashore over the caissons, over the road. In seven days the bridge had been completed. The LST could have gotten them up on the beach, but the LST would have been shot to pieces, and the crews did very well getting them over the pontoon bridges. They had lots of artillery, and they didn't have to worry about stepping into water over their heads. We landed them and got them on the bridge, and they walked ashore and went to where they were supposed to go and got there safely.

John T. Mason, Jr.: Why did some Americans insist on criticizing that installation?

Admiral Moran: They weren't there to see it. I think that Eisenhower thought it was a great job to do it that way. I think that the Navy fellows who saw it—Admiral King saw it, and he thought it was a great adventure.

John T. Mason, Jr.: Jimmy Hall didn't think it was great; I don't know why.

Admiral Moran: It would have been impossible to have gotten the magnitude across.

John T. Mason, Jr.: The great storm came along around the 19th of June, and that destroyed the American beach of Mulberries, didn't it?

Admiral Moran: Yes, but we just put two together and continued, and by that time—from the sixth—for two weeks we had been getting people ashore. I went over there on the 23rd, four days after it was hit, and the thing was working fine. Couldn't have been better.

John T. Mason, Jr.: Do I understand correctly that the British Mulberry beach was not affected by the storm, and it wasn't destroyed?

Admiral Moran: That's right. They had cover. They had rock shelter which protected them from the direction of the storm.

John T. Mason, Jr.: How long did those Mulberries continue to operate?

Admiral Moran: They continued to operate until, I think, about Christmastime. They still used the tugs. I don't know how long they used the Mulberries; they got to Antwerp, which was the great thing, got to Cherbourg. I went to Cherbourg. They lost two very good officers in an ambush in Cherbourg about the 26th or 27th of June.[*]

John T. Mason, Jr.: That was an ever-present danger in Cherbourg. Sullivan told me the story of the clearing of the harbor.[†] That was quite a task.
    Now will you tell me about your own personal activity from the day of the launching of the landing operation.

---

[*] See Quentin R. Walsh, "The Capture of Cherbourg," in *Assault on Normandy: First-Person Accounts from the Sea Services* (Annapolis: Naval Institute Press, 1994), pages 194-202.
[†] Commodore William A. Sullivan, USNR, was one of the Navy's top salvage experts during the war.

Admiral Moran: I considered my first job to keep morale at the highest possible pitch, because they never knew when we might get an air raid or we'd get one of these buzz bombs. I was around with the people; the procedures had been well established. We would send our tugs over to Selsey for the kind of craft we wanted to tow, depending on what they were ordering us from the beach, the far shore. We would give the crews when they came back much in the way of relief of the ordeal that they had suffered when they went over there. So that they'd go back again, feeling that when they came back again to us, they would have a glad hand—that we would be happy to see them and give them whatever we could in the way of relief and good food, time off—except when an emergency came. It was my job, having convinced the British as to the method that we were pursuing in getting the equipment over there, to make the tug selection. The first tug that I selected was a Dutch tug.

John T. Mason, Jr.: You mean from Allied sources?

Admiral Moran: Because it seemed to me that if you took a fellow whose country had been overrun, who was safe here, he would be the ideal man to go, rather than someone who had been in an easier job or who had been suffering all the way along from the blitzes and whatever else. Here was a man who was safe at home in England rather than being in Holland, where they were up against it. Somebody willing to go and who could go—he was an exceptionally good man, a good seaman, done lots of long-distance towing. The next fellow I sent was an American guy. I just talked to him; he is now president of one of our companies in Baltimore. He was a game sort of guy.

John T. Mason, Jr.: When did this selection process take place?

Admiral Moran: Four or five days before we left. I had to nominate the tug that was to do it. Selsey Beach would tell us there were two caissons ready to go. I selected this Dutchman in the British tug, and I sent our man, Hughes. They went over, and when they got there nobody knew what to do with them or where to put them or what, but they finally got settled; they found a place to do it. Then it got sort of commonplace. There was only one who, after having made the first trip, said to me, "I can't make another; I can't stand it; I want to go home."

I said, "Okay, go home."

John T. Mason, Jr.: War nerves?

Admiral Moran: Yes. Another guy, an engineer whose teeth went sour on him all of a sudden. I sent him to a place to get his teeth fixed, and he found something else instead of telling the truth. And I said, "You go back on that tug and make that trip, or I'll follow you around the world."

John T. Mason, Jr.: "I'll haunt you." And did it?

Admiral Moran: Yes.

John T. Mason, Jr.: And that was all it took.

Admiral Moran: Some nights when there was a bad raid, I would myself go out on the tug and sleep with the fellows. There was a guy up there whose name was Dan Hayman. He was a wild guy, a captain. He was a great ladies man, and the British had a lot of WRNS around, of course, and some of the British officers got fascinated by different WRNS. This fellow wanted to take some of them along. "Nothing doing," I said. "No women on deck."

He said, "The British got them."

And I said, "The British know what to do with them." So I didn't let them go. But these guys had a relaxed way about them.

John T. Mason, Jr.: You must have, because this comment comes up. You know that report from Admiral Little, and I am going to read that into the tape right at this point.[*]

---

[*] Admiral Sir Charles Little, RN, Commander in Chief Portsmouth.

This is from Admiral Sir Charles Little, August 11, 1944, to Admiral Stark. He speaks about your great administrative ability and then says a review of our services will be made part of an official report that the British will submit. Then he says:

> "I would like to take the opportunity of paying this tribute to him [Moran} and to thank you [Stark] for having made him available to us at such an important period. His charming personality goes without saying, and we are indeed sorry to part with him on this score alone."

Quite a statement from a British admiral, I would say. You must have had quite a winning way with someone.

Admiral Moran: We used to work pretty late over there with daylight saving time, double daylight saving time. Eleven o'clock at night was nothing, and the fellows who would come back from the far shore in France would go ashore and have a nice evening for themselves.

On one occasion three of them came back, and they each had a bouquet of flowers. They had been having a good strong pleasant evening, and they wanted to give me these flowers. I took them and said, "Wherever did you get the flowers at this hour?" Well, they said they stopped off at the cemetery and picked these flowers for me. They just enjoyed working with a towboat man. They said these were the best orders they ever got. Nobody was writing everything out, telling them exactly what to do. I just told them where to go and how to get there as best they could. And such a thing as rank was not evident at all.

John T. Mason, Jr.: You were a happy blend then of a civilian, a knowledgeable civilian and also a Navy man.

Admiral Moran: It never occurred to me that it was so hard, because the spirit of the British was really great. The British officers were outstanding—great people, polite. When we first got there, I called someone. The answer would be, "Loveband here," and right into the conversation. After I was there for a couple of months, he would say, "Loveband here."

I would say, Good morning, Captain. How are you today?" Well, nobody had ever done that in Great Britain—ask another officer how he was or what day it was or anything else. It was superiors and inferiors.

I went to the Naval War College here in Newport maybe eight or nine years after this operation, and there was a meeting of different groups. Before the meeting you were asked to express your previous wartime experience. I said, "My name is Moran."

The officer said, "What were your duties in the last World War?"

I said, "I had a number of duties, but probably the most important thing I had to do was in connection with the invasion of Normandy. I had a small part of that, and it went off quite well I thought."

Someone from the back of the room popped up and said, "He didn't have a small part of that; he had one of the biggest parts there were. I was there, and I saw it." I looked in the back; it was a submarine commander who'd come ashore and worked for Admiral Stark. Well, he overdid it, you see. But I didn't try to make it anything heroic.

Jack Franklin, the Army general, said to me, "Well, the Army certainly wants to give you a present, give you a decoration."

"Oh," I said, "I have a decoration. I got one from the Navy. I got one from the British and one from the French. I don't need any more. I don't want any more decorations."

"Ahh," he said, "come on."

"No," I said, "forget it."

But from then on he called me "Hero." Everywhere I saw him, "Hello, hero." But I didn't want it for that reason. I didn't think there was enough to this. I thought I was going under false colors, because all the things I did were just a continuation of things I had been doing.

John T. Mason, Jr.: Yes, but at the same time you had an appreciation of the importance of this operation.

Admiral Moran: And I didn't stand a good chance of being killed either; I knew that.

I don't know if I told you the story about going across on the *Queen Mary* and asking to get ashore before the troops got ashore.[*]

John T. Mason, Jr.: No, you didn't.

Admiral Moran: Well, we got into Gourock, Scotland, but the crew, the soldiers, the Army, and the nurses—they had 800 nurses and 14,000 troops and about 15 or 20 naval officers on the ship. And I had orders to get to London with all possible speed when I was going to Stark. The American port officer said, "You can't get off today."

"Why?" I said.

He said, "You have to go down with the troops tomorrow."

"Well," I said, "look, here are my orders."

And he said, "All right, if you want to get off, but you'll have to find your own way alone."

I said, "All right, get me off; I'll take my bags and go."

So they got me off, and I went up to Glasgow, which was right near, and I went to the railroad station. I said, "Do you have a train down to London tonight?" Yes, they had a train, and he mentioned the name of it. I said, "I'd like to have a ticket and would like a room if I could get it. I've just come across from America and am a little tired."

"Well, maybe we can get you that too," he said.

So he went inside, came out with the ticket for the room and transportation, and I said, "Thank you very much."

And he said, "That will be [whatever it was]."

So I said, "I don't have any money."

He said, "You don't have any money?"

"No," I said. "I just came from New York, and I haven't been paid my transportation. And I have no orders to go back, nothing." I just had the orders that I had to go over there.

He said, "We can't take you without any money."

---

[*] RMS *Queen Mary* was a large British passenger liner converted for use as a fast troop transport in World War II. She was built by John Brown & Company, Clydebank, Scotland; her first voyage as a commercial ship was in August 1936.

I said, "Why not? Isn't the American Navy here?"

But he said, "How? Everybody pays their fare."

I said, "There must be some way of getting me to London. We have Lend-Lease. Can you take me down on Lend-Lease or Lease-Lend, or whatever?"*

He said, "I don't think so."

"Ask somebody," I said.

So he went away again. He came back in 15 minutes and said, "All right, we'll take you." He put me on the train about 5:00 o'clock, and off I went. An American outfit met me down at whatever the station was, brought me to the wrong hotel, changed, and brought me to the right one. I had a room, a settee, and everything, very nice, and another room besides the bedroom. "What am I doing with this?" I said.

"Oh," he said, "you will probably have a lot of people come in and see you and all that sort of thing."

"Well, anybody can come and see me in here," I said. "I don't need this. Are we paying a big price for it. Get me another room."

John T. Mason, Jr.: You still didn't have any money in your pocket?

Admiral Moran: I didn't have any money at all, didn't have anything.

When Eisenhower told me to go over there to London—I had gone across the channel with Ike on a destroyer. One day after the storm I was told to report to Portsmouth at 5:00 o'clock in the morning. At 5:00 o'clock in the morning I was there, and I asked the British officer of the day what I was to do.

He said, "You are going out on a destroyer."

"Where is the destroyer going?"

He said, "I don't know." I went out on the *Thompson*, and I asked the officer of

---

* The Lend-Lease Act, passed by the U.S. Congress on 11 March 1941, was a device that enabled the United States to provide military aid to Great Britain without intervening directly in the European war then in progress. The program was later expanded to include aid to other Allied nations as well.

the deck if I could get some breakfast, because I hadn't any.*

So he said, "Sure, go down to the wardroom; they'll fix you up." So I went down to the wardroom and sat down at a table for two. Pretty soon a fellow came along, sitting alongside me as you are now. I looked at him, and it was Eisenhower.

So I said, "Good morning, General."

He said, "Can I get some breakfast here?"

I said, "Sure, just a minute. Mine is coming." So when mine came, I said, "Won't you take this?"

"No, no," and he said to the messman, "Get me [whatever]. So the messman came along with his breakfast.

We were talking, and I said, "General, when I came over here, my little daughter assumed that I would see you, and, based upon that assumption, she asked me if I could get your autograph, but I never thought that I would see you. I told her that if by chance I did, I would ask for it, so I hereby request your autograph if it is consistent with your wishes."

"Oh, sure." He wrote out his autograph, and I put it in my pocket. And he said, "We are going to have a meeting later on this morning, after breakfast, and I want to talk to you." So we went up into the wheelhouse and talked things over.

John T. Mason, Jr.: And what was the substance of the conversation?

Admiral Moran: The subject was the need for more equipment, because he was afraid—his army was then at St. Lo. It was only two weeks after the invasion, and he thought, "God, if they get pushed back again, how can I ever supply them?" I think Bradley was pushing him, too, for more reserves. So he said, "We have to send more equipment over there, and this stuff that we've got may not last, and we'll probably need more. I'm sending this cable to King and Land and Marshall, and I want you to go over tonight."

---

* USS *Thompson* (DD-627) was active in providing naval gunfire during the landings at Normandy. On 12 June she carried a group of VIPs from England to the invasion beaches at Normandy. Included were General George C. Marshall, General Dwight D. Eisenhower, Admiral Ernest J. King, and General Henry H. Arnold.

John T. Mason, Jr.: Back to the States?

Admiral Moran: Back to the States—no orders, no nothing. He said, "I'll tell Beetle Smith to arrange for your transportation and send you over."* So he met me back on the beach about 4:00 o'clock, and we went back to the destroyer. I went up to Prestwick the next morning, took a flight over to Reykjavik, Iceland, and then we went down to Greenland in a hell of a snowstorm, and then we flew to Washington.

Then I saw Marshall and King. King said to me, "I saw that place you built there at Normandy, and I must say it was a great job. Well, I got a lot of credit but for some of the phases of it that I had nothing much to do with. People who lived out where we were put this thing—the people who did it, who manned it, who put that stuff in shape, and we would never have gotten it done without Bassett. Bassett got a Bronze Star from the Navy, and he should have gotten something from the Army, but he didn't. In retrospect, I devised the whole landing craft system for getting the floats and barges ashore. I got some nice letters from the various generals, but I probably made a mistake in not taking the decoration. But I didn't do it, because I didn't want to be crowned.

John T. Mason, Jr.: Now, to complete the story, Ike sent you back to the States, and you conferred with the leaders about the re-order of these car floats and so forth. That was put into operation. Then you returned, and this is the time you came back on the *Queen Mary*?

Admiral Moran: No, I went over on the *Queen Mary*.

John T. Mason, Jr.: The first time you went over, you went on the *Queen Mary*.

Admiral Moran: Yes, the other times I flew.

John T. Mason, Jr.: But here you were, and the reason for lapping back was you were in London, in this hotel room—in the suite—and you didn't have any money.

---

* Lieutenant General Walter Bedell Smith, USA, was Eisenhower's chief of staff.

Admiral Moran: No, I didn't have any money. When I got back, they handed me the full check.

John T. Mason, Jr.: Got back to London?

Admiral Moran: With travel money and everything, and I said, "Well, I didn't pay anything. I didn't pay any money to travel." They had put me down daily expense and also travel. So I said, "I can't accept this. I traveled with the plane going over and traveled on the plane coming back. I didn't spend any money anywhere." I borrowed $15.00 or $20.00 from my wife; that's about all I had. I've never been known to carry any.

John T. Mason, Jr.: Oh, you don't carry any money. What's the personal reason for that?

Admiral Moran: I never gave it much thought.

John T. Mason, Jr.: That's a good reason. Anyway, here you were in London without any money, in a hotel suite and trusting in the Good Lord that it would be paid for. That was when you got back to London?

Admiral Moran: When Admiral King saw me, he said, "You look pretty worn out to me."
    I said, "We worked pretty hard over there."
    He said, "When are you going back?"
    I said, "Right away."
    "Well," he said, "look, you go over and see Admiral Land."
    So I went over and saw Admiral Land, and he said to me, "I hear you are going off on leave."
    "No," I said, "I'm going back."

He said, "You've got ten days' leave until after the Fourth of July. I left there on the 23rd and got back the 24th of June.

I said, "I never heard of such a thing."

He said, "Well, I've heard of it."

I said, "I don't have any orders to that effect."

He said, "You don't need any orders to that effect. Get out to the La Guardia air base, and they will fly you right back." So I went over to La Guardia and went to the naval station there, told them my name. They said, "We know you." They put me on that plane, and it took off, flew me to Ireland.

John T. Mason, Jr.: This was after you took the ten days' leave?

Admiral Moran: Yes. Then I got down to London, and they handed me all this money for subsistence and air travel and all. I said, "I don't need that." So then I came back here.

John T. Mason, Jr.: That was at the end of your tour over there?

Admiral Moran: That was the end of my tour. I came back to Washington, and I went to the West Coast.

Interview Number 4 with Rear Admiral Edmond J. Moran, U.S. Naval Reserve (Retired)
Place: Admiral Moran's office in the World Trade Center, New York City
Date: Monday, 17 October 1977
Interviewer: John T. Mason, Jr.

John T. Mason, Jr.: Admiral, it's very nice to see you on this stormy, rainy day in October. There were several points that I thought we should elaborate upon in connection with the Normandy invasion. You, off tape, have just told me one of considerable importance, I think, the story of the 50 tugs that were built in America, in preparation for war activity. Would you proceed at this point?

Admiral Moran: Yes. The United States War Shipping Board, before the creation of the War Shipping Administration, contracted for the construction of 50 oceangoing tugs, which were to be used for towing the concrete barges, which were to be built for the transportation of petroleum products or other bulk cargoes on the coast and in the North Atlantic. The concrete barge construction did not proceed as fast as the tug construction. As a consequence, the 50 tugs were built and delivered before any of the concrete barges were finished. These 50 tugs came on the scene at a very appropriate time. The Navy was very short of tugs, and the magnitude of the Shipping Board fleet of Liberty ships and others required the use of ocean tugs to meet the need for towing vessels which were disabled or damaged as a result of enemy action.*

John T. Mason, Jr.: Admiral, all of this was in the year approximately 1943?

Admiral Moran: Early in '43. As a result of the Maritime Commission's investigation, it was decided to assign the tugs, as they came out, to an operator who was equipped by experience and facility to handle the tugs, to operate them, and to assign them to business

---

* The Liberty ship was a mass-produced cargo ship designed by the U.S. Maritime Commission for use by the Allies in World War II. All told, American shipyards built 2,770 Liberties. The standard Liberty was 442 feet long, 57 feet in the beam, and had a light displacement of 3,337 tons. It had a cargo capacity of 10,920 deadweight tons. Maximum speed for a Liberty was about 12 knots.

which they could safely and efficiently handle. The Navy wished to acquire, by title, a percentage of the 50 tugs. When a discussion was had on this subject, it was shown that the tugs were built for a merchant crew, and a merchant crew to man one of these would consist of 20 to 25 seamen and officers.

John T. Mason, Jr.: These vessels were all uniform in size, were they?

Admiral Moran: These vessels were uniform in every respect.

John T. Mason, Jr.: What was their tonnage?

Admiral Moran: They were about 200 feet long, and they were about 2,500 horsepower.

John T. Mason, Jr.: I see

Admiral Moran: If the Navy had taken the vessels, it is probable—and almost certain—that they would man the vessels with as many as 100 personnel, consistent with Navy manning. The tugs were about of the same general description as the Navy ATA. When the subject had been fully discussed, it was determined that the tugs ought to remain under civilian management and civilian manning and assigned to perform such towage as the Navy would require, wherever it was required.

John T. Mason, Jr.: That was Admiral Land's decision?

Admiral Moran: Admiral Land's decision, along with the Assistant Chief of Naval Operations. As a consequence, when it was known what the requirements for the invasion of Normandy would be in the way of the need for tugs, seven of the Maritime Commission tugs, which were known as V-4s, were assigned to Operation Mulberry and to be engaged in the towage of caissons from the British coast to the Normandy beaches. They performed this service notably.

John T. Mason, Jr.: And with that quite diminished civilian crew?

Admiral Moran: With that largely diminished civilian crew.

John T. Mason, Jr.: Would you divert the story for a moment and tell me why there is such a large discrepancy between the civilian crew—found adequate for operating a tug like that efficiently—and the Navy crew, which is about three time or four times as much?

Admiral Moran: The Navy requires three times as many men to operate one of their tugs comparable to a merchant tug because the naval vessel is regarded first as a combat vessel, and consideration is always given to the possibility of enemy action resulting in the loss of the crew. The Navy does not have the restriction of financing the operation of the tug, and the naval personnel is not as experienced as the commercial tug. The commercial tug is at work all the while; that doesn't apply to the Navy tug. The cost of the Navy for a crew of enlisted men is probably less than the cost of the merchant tug's crew.

John T. Mason, Jr.: With their union scale of pay?

Admiral Moran: Not only their union scale of pay but with other costs not related to operations.

John T. Mason, Jr.: Well, sir, we have reached a point in the story where the Navy wanted some of these tugs, but it was ultimately decided, after adequate consultation, that they would be handed over to a commercial tug firm for management and operation. Now, would you tell me how a selection would be made as to the concern that would do this?

Admiral Moran: Admiral Land's office made inquiries as to the possibility of engaging managers and operators for these tugs, and since in the United States there had not been a great need for a large number of oceangoing tugs, there were, as a consequence, but few tug owners who were interested in managing long-distance towing. There was one company on the West Coast which handled most of the ocean towing. When they were asked if they would be willing to manage a number of ocean tugs for the War Shipping Administration, they declined. They said it was simply because they didn't have the spare personnel.

John T. Mason, Jr.: And that concern was Crowley?

Admiral Moran: That concern was Crowley. But they did accept the management and operation of one of the V-4 tugs.

John T. Mason, Jr.: They had a tremendous amount of work out of San Francisco.

Admiral Moran: They did; they were very busy, and they didn't have tugs that were as large as the V-4 tug, which required a more substantial crew than they used on their tugs. There were two companies in the Gulf of Mexico who couldn't possibly manage or operate V-4 tugs, simply because they did not have the personnel to do it. They offered to help in whatever way they could and were very energetic about performing the services with the tugs they had and which were capable of doing what they needed to do.

John T. Mason, Jr.: I take it that their operations were normally limited to the Gulf of Mexico?

Admiral Moran: Limited to the Gulf of Mexico and tributary waters.

John T. Mason, Jr.: These two concerns were what?

Admiral Moran: Quayle and Schmidt. On the East Coast there were several tug owners who had smaller oceangoing tugs, smaller than the V-4s, and they were engaged principally in towing barges laden with coal and in one case, lumber. When the German submarines appeared on the East Coast, these people were not able to operate due to the menace. They were unready to take on the management and operation of the war shipping fleet.

John T. Mason, Jr.: They were located where? Were they all concentrated in New York?

Admiral Moran: No, they were located in Philadelphia, Baltimore, and Jacksonville.

John T. Mason, Jr.: The fact remains that at that time and continuing so, the Moran Company was the largest of all, wasn't it?

Admiral Moran: Yes, the Moran Company was the largest of all engaged in miscellaneous, commercial, overseas towing. We had experience in delivering equipment to Venezuela, to North Africa, and to the United Kingdom at times. We had towed dredges, dry docks, and ships from the East Coast to the West Coast and conducted the only oceangoing service on the Atlantic Coast and became eligible therefore to take on the operation of the V-4 tugs.

John T. Mason, Jr.: This must be a matter of some embarrassment to you, because you were actively engaged in the Maritime Commission operations.

Admiral Moran: It was. I had nothing whatever to do with compensation for the services. As a matter of fact, I recommended that whatever was done by Moran would be done at Moran's cost and no profit would accrue from it. This matter was dealt with entirely outside of any consideration on my part. I am sure that there was no substantial profit made as a result of the agreement which was concluded by the Maritime Commission.

John T. Mason, Jr.: Would you tell me about your conversations with Lewis Douglas, who was the deputy, was he?

Admiral Moran: Lewis Douglas was the Deputy War Shipping Administrator.* As these tugs became available, and as the Navy continued to interest themselves in acquiring some, we discussed the position which the War Shipping Administration ought to take. It was agreed after full consideration that the War Shipping Administration should continue the management of the tugs operated under contract with suitable operators. Mr. Douglas knew, and Admiral Land knew, that an effort had been made to locate operators who had sufficient background and operating personnel and decided that they would make an independent declaration on a suitable operator, or suitable operators if there were more than one available.

John T. Mason, Jr.: And, as it turned out, Moran operated 49?

Admiral Moran: Forty-nine tugs.

John T. Mason, Jr.: And Crowley took one.

Admiral Moran: Crowley took one.

John T. Mason, Jr.: Did Moran have sufficient personnel, or did you have to lay up some of your other equipment?

Admiral Moran: No, we had a source of personnel, and we had a source of training. The 50 tugs did not come all at once. So, with the cooperation of the labor unions, we instituted a training program and trained personnel under operating conditions. The first tugs took four or five people for training—apprentices almost—seamen, but apprentices so far as towing operation was concerned. The Seaman's Union gave us people, gave the

---

*Lewis W. Douglas was deputy administrator, May 1942 to March 1944. Douglas, a Democrat from Arizona, previously served in the House of Representatives from March 1927 until his resignation in March 1933. He served as Director of the Budget from March 1933 to August 1934.

Maritime Commission people from their training school at Sheepshead Bay to the tugs while they were in operation, and they learned as they went along.*

John T. Mason, Jr.: Tell me a little about that Sheepshead Bay training school. How long a period did a man spend there?

Admiral Moran: I really don't know how long the training period was for, but it was managed under very competent people. The most prominent person I know was Admiral George W. Wauchope. He had been a master of ships, and he trained deep-sea seamen over there. He was a very competent man; he later took command of a ship and saw service in the South Pacific.

John T. Mason, Jr.: Was there any problem with obtaining new personnel in that time, considering the fact that we had the draft in the country?

Admiral Moran: Well, these people, as I remember it, when they signed on were free from the draft as seamen. They had obtained seamen's papers.

John T. Mason, Jr.: And that was their wartime duty?

Admiral Moran: That was their wartime duty. It was far more risky than a lot of the others.

John T. Mason, Jr.: You told me off tape about the tremendous mileage accomplished by these various tugs. Would you put that on, please?

Admiral Moran: Yes, it is interesting to note, from the records, that the number of tows which these V-4 tugs successfully completed amounted to 1,153. In those tows the

---

* Shortly after Pearl Harbor, the U.S. Coast Guard purchased 125 acres of property on the eastern tip of Brooklyn, New York, for a huge training center. Seventy-six acres were used for the Sheepshead Bay Maritime Service station.

number of units was 1,568—that is to say, on some occasions two or three barges or whatever were towed.

John T. Mason, Jr.: That was the total for the 50 tugs.

Admiral Moran: The number of miles towed was 1,825,723 actual towage miles. The number of miles the tugs ran light—that is to say, without a tow in order to reach the destination where the tow was to be picked up—was 1,270,542 miles.

John T. Mason, Jr.: This sounds, Admiral, as though it encompassed the whole world. Give me some illustration of where these tugs went.

Admiral Moran: One of the earliest tows consisted of a V-4 tug and three barges loaded with lubricating oil from Tampa, Florida, to New Caledonia, the port of Nouméa, by way of the Panama Canal. That was the first tow. Thereafter, equipment was towed almost everywhere in the Southwest Pacific. Dry docks known as sectional docks, ABSDs—advance base sectional docks—were towed mainly from the West Coast to New Caledonia, Manus, Espiritu Santo, Kwajalein, Eniwetok. Dredges were towed to Nouméa, to Guam to deepen the entrance to the harbor at Guam. Alaska, from the West Coast mainly, barges to Alaska; they were dropped off and drifted onto the beaches where they were used. The tugs couldn't approach close enough to the beaches to secure the barges that they towed, so the barges were simply towed to about where they were needed, and they drifted on to the beach and were unloaded on the beach. Towed to Europe, mainly, of course, to British ports: Cardiff, Newcastle, Plymouth, Portsmouth. Disabled ships were picked up at sea and brought safely into port—merchant vessels torpedoed or machinery disablement.

John T. Mason, Jr.: That, in the aggregate, was an heroic operation, and it must have put an awful burden on the civilian personnel.

Admiral Moran: It did, it did. They were paid well, but they really performed particularly well at Normandy, where they were under fire at least for the first ten days of the invasion, and they were in no way independently able to defend themselves against air attack or, as a matter of fact, from an E-boat attack. E-boats were in the channel, anxious to do all the damage they could; there was surface protection and air protection as well, but, despite that, two of the tugs in the invasion were torpedoed. Fortunately, none of the War Shipping tugs were lost; there were one Navy tug and one British tug.

John T. Mason, Jr.: With this worldwide operation and the hazardous areas where they operated—Alaska and other places—there must have been some casualties to the tugs, were there?

Admiral Moran: There were no casualties to the tugs; there was a tug lost while it was in tow in the Pacific. The need for small tugs in the Pacific ports was met by 85-foot tugs not capable of getting to the destination under their own power. They lacked fuel capacity, and they lacked the seagoing quality that would have permitted self-navigation. One of these tugs in tow was lost, broke away from the tug towing and was lost, foundered.

John T. Mason, Jr.: Were there any problems with the personnel. With the civilians being subjected to war conditions, were all of them able to stand up under this?

Admiral Moran: They stood up well, considering what they were up against. There was only one master who asked to be relieved after his first trip to the Normandy invasion. He just couldn't accomplish the task; he was an older man, and I think his age had more to do with his asking for relief than anything else. He couldn't stand the number of hours on watch. Tugs were taking about a day and a half of constant difficulty in crossing from Portsmouth or Selsey Beach to France. About a day and a half, sometimes two, depending on the weather and depending upon how the tow stood together. And that was too much for some of the fellows who were older.

John T. Mason, Jr.: That's certainly understandable. Since these were civilian crews, if anything had materialized in the way of disorder among the crews, how were they to be controlled? I know the Coast Guard set up immediate courts or something to consider problems with personnel. These were set up in Britain and all over the world actually; would the tug crews have come under their jurisdiction?

Admiral Moran: I am sure, if the occasion required, they would have. Yes, because there were Coast Guard personnel. Everywhere we based, or almost everywhere we went, we would find Coast Guard personnel. I don't know of a single occasion where it was necessary to appeal to the Coast Guard for help in the case of personnel difficulties.

John T. Mason, Jr.: That was a remarkable record. I think it was probably the largest enterprise that even Moran had ever undertaken.

Admiral Moran: Oh, sure. There were about 2,500 men involved. Each tug had a gun crew, too, you know, supplied by the Navy.

John T. Mason, Jr.: That was a military gun crew, protection against air perhaps?

Admiral Moran: Air defense mainly. Of course, I suppose if they saw a submarine they'd shoot at it.

John T. Mason, Jr.: These tugs were under a contract to Moran, and when the contract expired where did the tugs go?

Admiral Moran: The tugs were returned to the lay-up fleets on the West Coast and the East Coast. The Hudson River, Mobile, James River, the West Coast in the vicinity of San Francisco, and also in Seattle.

John T. Mason, Jr.: They were put into mothballs, were they?

Admiral Moran: Yes.

John T. Mason, Jr.: Is that where they remain now?

Admiral Moran: To the best of my knowledge, that's where they are.

John T. Mason, Jr.: That sounds like a waste.

Admiral Moran: I don't think anybody wants them, because the power requirements have increased so since that time.

John T. Mason, Jr.: They did such yeoman service in the wartime, they would probably be worn out.

Admiral Moran: They were expensive to run, very costly to run—the machinery problem.

John T. Mason, Jr.: They were diesel powered?

Admiral Moran: Yes, they were diesel powered, but the modern diesel engine is nothing like what they were equipped with, really, and the separate engine rooms that they had—bulkheads required, personnel on both sides of these damage-proof bulkheads. They were expensive tugs to operate.

John T. Mason, Jr.: That was certainly a laudable enterprise. I can see why at the outset you were somewhat embarrassed, because your own name was attached to the firm that took the contract.

Admiral Moran: The main embarrassment that I had in connection with the Normandy invasion grew out of my assignment. Admiral Stark wanted me to go over to London to look at the plans for moving the units of the artificial harbors from Great Britain to

Normandy. He wanted to be sure, or as sure as he could be made, that the plans which had been designed for moving the units were practical and could be made without unreasonable difficulty.

When I arrived in London, a meeting was called by Admiral Ramsay to discuss with me the manner in which the operation was to be conducted, from beginning to end, every phase of it. I made some suggestions with respect to gear, and I thought that other than that and the possibility of a shortage of tugs becoming necessary as a result of enemy action, it seemed to me that the deliveries ought to have been made without too much difficulty. A British captain had been appointed to supervise the event and all of its activities.

After this meeting, the British admiral, an assistant to Admiral Ramsay, who was the Allied Naval Commander in Chief, suggested that I be assigned to the job of supervising and conducting the total job. Admiral Stark's interest was restricted to the American bases, so he was asked if he would be willing to assign me to the task of dealing with the needs of the British bases. That meant that I would be relieved of anything that I might be called upon to do for the American side of the delivery of the equipment.

Admiral Stark, under a suggestion from General Eisenhower, directed that I be given the job that the Allied Naval Commander in Chief wanted me to take. The British officer who was to have had charge of the job was glad to be relieved, because he didn't feel competent to deal with the problems that might arise. He was a seagoing officer who had no experience whatever in towing or managing towing operations. And since there was some evidence that I had what was regarded as the experience necessary to carry out this mission, I be appointed to take the job over. And I did that about a month and a half before the invasion took place, so I had time to become acquainted with the British officers, and to admire them, as well as their American counterparts.

John T. Mason, Jr.: I would say not too much time, if it was only a month and a half.

Admiral Moran: There was a communication between Admiral Stark and Admiral Land at the outset of the decision to put me in charge, because Admiral Land had not agreed that I spend more than maybe ten days in Europe. Finally, communications continued, and the matter was settled. I was to try to do the job, and I did, with the help of a capable friend named Sam Loveland of Philadelphia. He looked after many of the difficult problems.

John T. Mason, Jr.: What was his status?

Admiral Moran: He was associated with me in the War Shipping Administration, and he flew over to Lee on the Solent, where we were headquartered, and he was there for about a month at my request.*

John T. Mason, Jr.: Was he in uniform?

Admiral Moran: No, he wasn't. He came over as a civilian. I also had another officer with me named William Kirk.

John T. Mason, Jr.: Alan Kirk's brother.

Admiral Moran: He was very helpful, very ambitious, and anxious to do all he could. He was a lieutenant commander. I also had the help of a British lieutenant commander named Kenneth Poland. He was duty officer and a very good one.

John T. Mason, Jr.: These men constituted your staff?

Admiral Moran: Yes.

John T. Mason, Jr.: How did you assemble this staff so quickly?

Admiral Moran: They were there, but in some respects they were doing the wrong job, so they had to do the job that I thought they could more competently perform.

---

* The Solent is a channel extending between the Isle of Wight and the mainland of southern England.

John T. Mason, Jr.: How did you put your finger on these competent men?

Admiral Moran: By talking to them, discussing the jobs to be done. The hours were frightful—around the clock. One day before the invasion we had a visitor from SHAEF who asked us how things were going along.* We told him we were going along very well, we were working hard. He said, "How are communications?"

"Communications are perfect; we can't get in touch with anybody, and nobody can get in touch with us."

John T. Mason, Jr.: Was there any problem in assembling these concrete caissons?

Admiral Moran: No. They worked perfectly.

John T. Mason, Jr.: They were manufactured where?

Admiral Moran: They were manufactured in Great Britain.

I should say a word about Captain Bassett, although I think I referred to him before. He had the difficult task of placing these caissons precisely where they were intended to be placed, and that was a difficult job under fire. He was spectacular; he managed these Army tugs, civilian manned by people who weren't trained for the work at all. But he was there in constant attendance, watching the thing carefully, showing them how do to it, telling them precisely what to do, when to do it. And that's what did the job. I knew what needed to be done, but the first thing that I needed were people who knew how to do what needed to be done. I was nothing more than a fairly efficient manager.

John T. Mason, Jr.: An administrator of the whole project.

You must have, and obviously throughout your career you have demonstrated that fact, the ability to select the right men for the right jobs.

---

* SHAEF—Supreme Headquarters Allied Expeditionary Force.

Admiral Moran: If I had any ability at any time to do anything, I think it has been the power to convince a competent person that he had the capacity to perform very difficult tasks. The best men are the best trained men to accomplish difficult feats that they have never tried before.

John T. Mason, Jr.: The training is the background. But some men have adequate training and still aren't able to perform to the peak.

Admiral Moran: Then it becomes the task of the manager to convince the person that he can do it.

John T. Mason, Jr.: That he has that ability to rise to the peak.

Admiral Moran: That he can do it. We got very fond of each other—the captains of the tugs. I had four stripes, and they had two or none or whatever. But in that kind of an operation, where the risk was at times fairly high, it took, I think, confidence in the man who was assigned to do the job that the person who proposed it felt he could take the risk and do it. I remember one evening about 11:00 o'clock at night three of the British captains came in to see me. It was almost daylight then, too, and they each had a bouquet of flowers. They had been at their local pub undoubtedly, and they also had attended the wake of one of their colleagues. When they put the flowers on the desk they said, "Jerry sent these to you." Jerry was the man who was killed in the action. I think that tells a great deal about how the thing went over.

John T. Mason, Jr.: It says volumes about the kind of relationship you were able to establish with your skippers.

Admiral Moran: When the going was tough out there, we had one captain, a dear fellow; his name was Dan Hayman. We'd get these fellows dropping bombs at night and also those buzz bombs, and the crews would get nervous, so I would go out and sleep on the tug and come in in the morning. We'd have a good time talking with the officers. And shrapnel would come down; we thought nothing of it.

John T. Mason, Jr.: You considered this a part of leadership?

Admiral Moran: Well, yes. I had no background or education that enabled me to think I was a great guy doing something. I was just interested in helping out.

John T. Mason, Jr.: But you knew the value of leadership in a military sense, and since you had been in World War I and had a brush with it then.

Admiral Moran: Yes, but I really don't think there is much difference between life in the business world or in the military service. In the long run, and as a general thing, I admire the Navy—the way they train their officers to become leaders, to become strong men, wise, thoughtful, persuasive, tolerant, compassionate. I think that's why we have been so successful in the troubles we have had, because we have had those kinds of people. True, as in life everywhere and under all circumstances, we have unreasonable people at times, but sooner or later—much sooner than later, I suppose—they are found out, and they're taken out of harm's way.

John T. Mason, Jr.: What percentage in the business world are of that nature, with those virtues and capacities?

Admiral Moran: To the extent of the success of the company, of the employer, I think that the country is great because the people are great. Nobody is perfect in disposition or in relationships, but I think that we have the best government and the best people running the government. I admire the people; I admire the naval officers, the strict naval officers, the fellow who calls you by your last name—it makes no difference to me. That's all right; he is trying. That's what he has been told to do, and he is doing it. I think the gentlest man I ever saw was Stark. And when I recall meeting Admiral King, I was pretty well scared. I thought, "By gosh, this is a tough fellow; he is going to ask me a lot of questions." He didn't ask me any questions. He opened a drawer of his desk and said, "Do you smoke?"

And I said, "Yes, I smoke once in a while."

"Have a cigarette." He closed the drawer and gave me a cigarette, and he said, "I thought you did a pretty good job over there."

"Well," I said, "I'm very grateful to you, Admiral, for having thought that."

He said, "What do you want?"

I said, "Admiral General Eisenhower sent you a dispatch which tells you what he wants."

He said, "Do you agree with it?"

I said, "I agree with the need, but I have nothing to do with how soon it can be obtained. It would be a difficult task in the wintertime or in the late fall."

John T. Mason, Jr.: This pertained to another convoy of car ferries and supplies to Europe to come in October.

Admiral Moran: Admiral King said that he would arrange for another convoy when the equipment was assembled on the East Coast. So I thanked him and left after he told me that he thought that I looked as though I needed a rest and ought to stay for a short period before returning back to England.

John T. Mason, Jr.: Since you mention Admiral King, in a previous interview you said that King had seen the Mulberries as they were installed. Were you with him on that occasion? When did he come over? What were the circumstances?

Admiral Moran: He came over to England and went out in the Channel and then went over to France and saw the artificial harbors in place and sent word for me to come to London to see him. I was out in the Channel and didn't get the word until the middle of the afternoon. I was driven up to London and went to the duty officer and asked why I had been sent for. He said, "Admiral King wanted to see you, but he had to leave; he couldn't wait." So I stayed overnight in London, through another air raid, and was back to the Solent the next morning.

John T. Mason, Jr.: In the previous interview you also referred to the fact that the great storm which happened shortly after the middle of June had destroyed the Mulberry installation at the American beaches, and then you said they just went ahead and put a couple of others together and went on. I wondered if you would elaborate on that? Where did the others come from? How did this happen?

Admiral Moran: What they did was mainly with the roadways, the pontoons that I have described. Many of the pontoons had been damaged and sank to the bottom, taking the pontoon line with them in part. The damaged ends were separated from the floating ends, and the line was simply shortened; it was much shorter than it was before. Some of the lines were almost 3,000 feet in length, and when they were shortened up, they became 1,800 feet or 2,000 feet, but by that time the movement had slowed down. The storm occurred the 19th, two weeks after—if it happened at the outset, before we had that stuff on the beach—the great thing was that these car floats could go right up on the beach with the cargo of gasoline, K rations, ammunition, or whatever, and sit there high and dry, come unloaded. And when the tide rose they were floated off and taken back for another load of whatever they wanted. There was nothing better. It was remarkable that that storm did not occur before it did.

John T. Mason, Jr.: It was providential that it held off, wasn't it?

Admiral Moran: I think we were supposed to go on the fourth, as I remember. And I decided on the basis of what the fellows were telling me that we had better not, so we delayed it until the sixth.

John T. Mason, Jr.: That was a previous storm of high waves and rough seas.

Admiral Moran: I didn't think that the storm was that bad.

John T. Mason, Jr.: Which one?

Admiral Moran: Either one.

John T. Mason, Jr.: You really didn't think they were that devastating?

Admiral Moran: No, not until I got over there and saw what happened on the beach.

John T. Mason, Jr.: Perhaps the effect of the storm on the English coast was somewhat different from what it was on the French coast, because the French coast was more exposed.

Admiral Moran: Sure. The wind came in from the west and south. I was thinking of these trips that we made, and the equipment was lightly constructed. They are not going to have any more of that stuff in any other hostility, I don't think. I was told that I was to have about the same job in Japan as I had over here in Normandy.

John T. Mason, Jr.: For the proposed invasion of the homeland?

Admiral Moran: Yes.

John T. Mason, Jr.: Fortunately, the job didn't materialize. You did tell me that you also visited Cherbourg during the time that they were in the process of clearing the harbor. Tell me a little more about that.

Admiral Moran: I went over there at Admiral Stark's instructions, and when I got there it was just after Patton had gone through.[*]

---

[*] Lieutenant General George S. Patton was an Army officer in World War II; he led the U.S. Third Army across Europe following the D-Day invasion in 1944.

John T. Mason, Jr.: Did you have a particular mission?

Admiral Moran: They wanted to know what was needed in the way of port equipment to discharge ships in case Antwerp didn't materialize, and they were going to route some of our stuff through the south into Germany. I made a survey and tried to put it on one piece of paper as to the number of barges and lighters and tugs that would be needed to do so much work.

John T. Mason, Jr.: The destruction was very great, wasn't it?

Admiral Moran: Yes. So the admiral thought I hadn't given much thought to it, because I could put it on one piece of paper. "Well," I said, "Admiral, I thought you wanted to know only what you needed to know. You asked me how much equipment would be needed to discharge vessels. You didn't tell me how many vessels there would be, or how much cargo there would be, or when the port would be ready to accept the size of ships that might be coming. This survey that I made contemplates approximately the same movement of cargo that goes through Utah and Omaha Beach."

He said, "Okay, that'll do." That was the end of him.

John T. Mason, Jr.: What more did he want?

Admiral Moran: I couldn't say; it was beyond me honestly.

John T. Mason, Jr.: You had been back to Washington, and then you returned to London again while the Normandy operation—or inland from Normandy—was under way. What was your mission when you returned to London? The initial landings had been accomplished, and supplies were getting in. What was your mission then?

Admiral Moran: I resumed what I had been doing before I left. Admiral Land was still inquiring of Admiral Stark as to when I would be returning. So Admiral Stark sent for me and asked me if I thought the work could be carried on successfully henceforth without my presence. I said, "Yes."

He said, "Fine, then I will give you orders to return."

John T. Mason, Jr.: Were you leaving Loveland there?

Admiral Moran: No, Loveland had left before I left. Loveland had left, I should think, about the middle of July.

John T. Mason, Jr.: The tugs were all still pulling away?

Admiral Moran: Sure.

John T. Mason, Jr.: Under whose supervision did you leave them then?

Admiral Moran: I left them under the supervision of a Britisher, Kenneth Poland. He was the nominal man there. It was a British operation, you see; it wasn't an American operation. When I left, Admiral Sir Charles Little knew about it, and Admiral Ramsay knew about it, and it was up to them to replace me. It wasn't up to Stark to replace me, because I wasn't Stark's man. He allowed me to go to the British.

John T. Mason, Jr.: I have always been not quite clear as to the scope of Admiral Stark's role there in Europe with these other active naval commanders under Eisenhower. Can you enlighten me? What function did he actually perform?

Admiral Moran: I think that Stark's position was Commander of the American Naval Forces in Europe. He was the commander of the force, just as Tedder was in command of the Air Force aspect and Bradley was commander of the Army, but Ike was the boss of the whole thing.* All of them—Bertram Ramsay, Tedder, Montgomery—all reported to

---

* Air Chief Marshal Arthur W. Tedder, RAF, Deputy Supreme Commander under Eisenhower.

Ike, and Ike was responsible for the whole thing.[*] Stark was responsible for the Navy, but he had task force commanders—Moon, Kirk.[†] Kirk was, I think, commander of the assault. He had the *Augusta*; that was his flag. And he had Moon, Hewitt, and other admirals.[‡]

John T. Mason, Jr.: And Stark, I take it, in some large measure had to be concerned about logistics.

Admiral Moran: Oh, yes, sure. But the task force commanders had to have their people, too, and Stark was responsible for logistics. I don't think if there was ever a test he would have had much to do with strategy and tactics.

John T. Mason, Jr.: That would have been purely operational, and he didn't have that.

Admiral Moran: Ramsay would have been in that, because I don't think you could have had a situation where Ike and his commanders would have been American way down to the staff on the force—the task force or whatever the Army does. When Patton got into slight difficulties, it was Eisenhower who dealt with him, nobody else. The other side of the thing was that when the British wanted to say something—Montgomery was a field commander; we had Marshall here—Marshall was only talking to Ike.

John T. Mason, Jr.: It was a complicated setup, because it was an Allied operation.

Admiral Moran: Sure, it was an Allied operation right straight down, and it really worked.

John T. Mason, Jr.: Did you have an opportunity to look up any old friends in Great Britain while you were there?

---

[*] Field Marshall Bernard Law Montgomery, ground commander under Eisenhower.
[†] Rear Admiral Don P. Moon, USN, Commander Task Force U for the assault on Utah Beach.
[‡] Vice Admiral H. Kent Hewitt, USN, Commander Western Naval Task Force for the invasion of Southern France in August 1944.

Admiral Moran: No, I never did any socializing. Once Admiral Ramsay took me out to dinner; that was a very nice thing to do. Those British people were very fine people, very concerned, very gracious. They knew we had the stuff that they needed to win the war, and they knew we had the people to carry out the tasks, and they dealt with them accordingly. They were just as considerate, gentle, and nice. Never had a hard word to say to me; of course, I was a pretty easy subject too.

John T. Mason, Jr.: Yes, I think you are rather much on the gentle side.

We were talking earlier about your philosophy on the cooperation that people give to a successful operation, and you said that this pertained also in the business world. I think it would be appropriate to make an observation that I made to your son last time—the fact that I have been here a number of times now and have discovered this very wonderful atmosphere among your employees. The fact that they are quite considerate, and they notice little things and so forth. It is an unusual atmosphere that I have observed, because I go many places. And he said that that largely sprang from your policies through the years.

Admiral Moran: I hope so. We're only here once, and you don't get a second chance. You have to persevere and try; it's only money. Your relationship with people is far greater than relationship with money. We have to be generous in every respect. I know lots of men—very cordial and gracious, but they have to be careful of the resources that are not theirs, and the result sometimes is that they are misjudged. They would be perfectly willing to give their own last possession to help anyone in need, but the custodianship of other people's property is a responsibility that can never be overlooked. That is the difference between the world of business and the social world.

Interview Number 5 with Rear Admiral Edmond J. Moran, U.S. Naval Reserve (Retired)

Place: Captain Searle's residence in Alexandria, Virginia

Date: Thursday, 21 September 1978

Interviewers: John T. Mason, Jr., and Captain Willard F. Searle, Jr., U.S. Navy (Retired)

John T. Mason, Jr.: Tell us about coastwise towing on the eastern coast in World War I. It was rather limited in scope, but there was some.

Admiral Moran: The coastwise transportation tug and barge business consisted of probably 30 or 35 seagoing tugs and probably 75 or 80 barges, of which many were converted sailing ships. They were engaged in the transportation of lumber from the South, Fernandina, Florida, Jacksonville, Charleston, and Savannah to the northeastern ports of New York and New England. There was the coal trade, which consisted of the transportation of bituminous coal from Hampton Roads and Philadelphia, and anthracite coal from Philadelphia and New York to all of the New England ports. Very little petroleum, refined or crude, was transported by barge during that time. These tugs were not seriously interfered with in the coastwise transportation business as a result of submarine warfare, with the exception of the tug *Perth Amboy*, which was shelled by a German submarine off Cape Cod.[*]

Captain Searle: That was the *U-52*?

Admiral Moran: I don't know if it was the *U-52*, which had already sunk one of the Red Cross liners bound from St. John's, Newfoundland, to New York.

Captain Searle: Was the Red Cross liner American flag or British?

Admiral Moran: She was British flag.

---

[*] The German submarine *U-156* damaged the tugboat *Perth Amboy* with gunfire on 21 July 1918 when she was operating in Nantucket Sound, three miles off Orleans, Massachusetts. The tugboat was salvaged and towed to port; her crew suffered no casualties.

Captain Searle: When the Germans shelled the *Perth Amboy* we weren't at war with them yet, were we?

Admiral Moran: They fired at the *Perth Amboy* after we became engaged in war with them.* But there were no serious submarine activities in 1918 that I can recall. Our tug and barge transportation was not seriously bothered.

Captain Searle: There was no real Navy rescue tug service. One of the reasons, I've always felt, was that there wasn't any radio communication for commercial tugs as a general rule, so there wasn't any opportunity to call for emergency assistance and get out there. The radiotelephone itself changed the nature of the rescue-towing business. In fact, it started the rescue-towing business.

Admiral Moran: I can't recall precisely the first radio-equipped tug capable of the transmission by voice of much more than 150 miles. I think there was some capability in Merritt-Chapman's *I. J. Merritt*. I think she could deal with radio communications—by voice and otherwise.

John T. Mason, Jr.: Was this during the war period, or was it a little later?

Admiral Moran: I'm pretty sure it was during the war period, but I am not certain that they carried any means of communication that were helpful in accomplishing salvage or conducting salvage between the ship and the salvage tug.

Captain Searle: That's my understanding of the rescue towing and the salvage business in the World War I era. There was the famous Rescue Salvage Company Foundation in Halifax and the Merritt-Chapman Company in New York. Their salvage ships in those days were, in fact, salvage tugs, and they were very proud of the fact that they carried lots of radio capabilities. It's only in the last two or three decades, from World War II

---

* The U.S. declaration of war was on 6 April 1917.

onward, that the rescue-towing business became a distinct thing from the salvage business. That, of course, is one of the things I want to develop here.

Admiral Moran: I would think that we had more to do with rescue salvage, as opposed to the salvage of a vessel that resulted in a distribution based upon factors that are no longer present, in the earlier days of salvage.

John T. Mason, Jr.: When you say "we," Admiral, you mean the Moran Company?

Admiral Moran: Yes, the Moran Company. We indicated a willingness to perform rescue salvage without the use of the word "salvage." We rendered a rescue service and based compensation upon a daily rate for the tug, and the rate was to be paid whether the rescue was effective or not. We did not deal with the value of the ship or the danger in which the vessel might find herself at the time the tug arrived at the site of the rescue.

John T. Mason, Jr.: That's quite a distinction, sir. How did you arrive at that policy?

Admiral Moran: Because it was clear to us at that time that the vessel, disabled, was certainly in no serious jeopardy. It was simply a matter of being unable to propel itself, had no means of turning the propeller which would give it progress. So we were doing nothing more than towing a dead ship from a place where there was no real danger involved to its existence or to its crew, its personnel.

It is, of course, correct that the job itself required a great degree of skill in handling during bad weather conditions, and the tug at times was unable to make connection for a period of heavy seas or gales of wind. But I can't think of a case where the rescue was not completed safely, the ship delivered to a safe harbor. I can think of no case where there was a failure to accomplish the mission.

Captain Searle: Let me respond to that. I think that's a good policy, but it presupposes that the Moran organization, in following that policy, only did rescue towing when it had a tug available. The opposite side of the coin is whether or not there will be rescue tugs

tugs positioned in ports, similar to fire engines positioned in firehouses around the neighborhood, standing by for a call. If a tug has to sit in port for months and months and years and years on end, becoming a burden to the overhead of the company, then I think it would be expected that somebody, either the government through a subsidy or some other means, has to pay for that protection represented by the tug again in port.

But, as I understand the policy you iterate, Admiral, you didn't make any commitments to the shipping industry to keep a tug standing by in Staten Island.

Admiral Moran: We simply represented that our fleet was sufficiently able in numbers and capacity to tow at many points on the Atlantic Coast. We never sought or represented that the units that we would propose to use were available and waiting for an opportunity to perform a rescue service outside of its regular operating activities.

Captain Searle: You're saying, then, that your firm was big enough, and your fleet of tugs was big enough that you had flexibility, that there was, in fact, always a tug available in the firehouse, and nobody had to subsidize it; the government didn't need to subsidize you.

John T. Mason, Jr.: Out on assignment and doing something else.

Admiral Moran: And we never misrepresented the location of the tug or the time required to reach and save those vessels.

John T. Mason, Jr.: Admiral, on the average, how many jobs of this sort were you called upon to do in a given year?

Admiral Moran: At the end of World War II the Liberty ships were losing propellers on frequent occasions, and I would not be surprised if we had as many as 15 calls during a year, to go varying distances off the coast to rescue a ship.

John T. Mason, Jr.: In biblical terms, you were serving as a Good Samaritan to disabled ship?

Captain Searle: Yes, that's certainly true. Between World War I and World War II, did the business of rescue towing increase? You said you had maybe 15 in the 1946-47 period when Liberties were in great abundance. When did you begin to do rescue-towing work, if you didn't do it in World War I?

Admiral Moran: I would think, without referring to records, that our earliest rescue service commenced in about 1934 or 1935. At that time we were operating steam tugs; they were towing on the coast and had limited endurance. For the most part, they were coal-burners, and the limitation of fuel capacity restricted getting too far in the Atlantic.

John T. Mason, Jr.: In other words, it became more feasible with the diesel?

Admiral Moran: With the diesel, yes.

John T. Mason, Jr.: It became long-legged then.

Admiral Moran: Yes.

Captain Searle: Was there any dialogue between you, as the president of Moran, and Captain Scott, president of Merritt-Chapman, and Scott, with relation to rescue towing and salvage?*

Admiral Moran: I don't think that Captain Scott felt happy with our rate structure for rescue. I never discussed the subject with him. I discussed it with Captain Davis, and Captain Davis's position was that if we could perform the service at a lower cost to an insurance company or a ship owner, he saw no reason why we shouldn't do it.

---

* Captain T. A. Scott.

Captain Searle: Was there a kind of gentlemen's agreement that Merritt and Davis themselves didn't get into the rescue-towing business, and Moran really wasn't interested in salvage?

Admiral Moran: No, there was no such thing. No.

John T. Mason, Jr.: Admiral, was the federal government interested in employing your services in this area?

Admiral Moran: I never detected any federal interest in us.

Captain Searle: I think that's right. It's one of the crazy things that federal interest in this business has always been focused on Merritt-Chapman, and Scott, or was always focused until last year on Merritt-Chapman, and Scott. The Navy's salvage contract goes back to World War I, but that's what I was leading into, whether or not you ever commented or grumbled to the federal government with respect to the subsidy, if you wish, the sweetheart contract, that the Navy had with Merritt-Chapman, and Scott, and then Merritt-Chapman, and Scott, and then Murphy Pacific.

Admiral Moran: We never had any discussion with the federal government on that subject.

Captain Searle: The interesting thing to me always was that when the present public statute, Public Law 513, 10 U.S. Code 7361, which is the law that was passed in about 1947, one which Admiral Sullivan had promoted, the hearings were generally favorable to the Navy's position, except that Tom Crowley, Sr., from San Francisco, made the effort to come all the way across country by train and raised holy hell in the public hearings that Congress held. But there was no comment. Moran was totally silent. Why was that, Admiral?

Admiral Moran: We had nothing to say about it. There was no reason for us to protest what anyone else was doing. We didn't seek any assistance from anybody. We felt entirely independent of the whole field. If there was a ship in trouble and we could get to it and bring it in safely, fine.

Captain Searle: And you didn't covet the business that Merritt-Chapman got?

Admiral Moran: Not by any means, no.

John T. Mason, Jr.: You were beginning to have more and more of your own, anyway.

Admiral Moran: Merritt-Chapman dominated the situation for a long, long time and unquestionably performed a commendable service. There's no doubt about that. They got the ships in, but the cost was something that we thought was important to underwriters and ship owners.

Captain Searle: Why did you always take the position that a tugboat company was a towing company, and a salvage company was a salvage company, and they were two separate things? You were not interested in the salvage business?

Admiral Moran: We couldn't perform in the salvage business on the basis that Merritt or any other salvage company operated on. We didn't have equipment standing by. Our great point was we had equipment capable of towing almost anywhere you wanted to go, or would go, at any time, without having the tremendous cost of equipment standing by waiting for something to happen.

John T. Mason, Jr.: I suppose, too, Admiral, from a practical point of view, two big organizations were located there in New York. One had its own problems, and the other had its own.

Captain Searle: Well, if I may put some words in the admiral's mouth, from a story that he has told me a time or two over the years in the very rewarding friendship that we have had, as far as I'm concerned, it's a very tenable position. You've told me in the past you felt that if Standard Oil Company had tankers coming in and out of New York Harbor, and they saw fit to do business with you, if they were a valued customer, or if the Cunard Line had their liners coming in and out of New York and you did their docking, and then a ship all of a sudden was in distress of Nantucket Shoals or Sandy Hook or someplace, and they asked you for assistance, it would have been not only bad business but certainly ludicrous for you all of a sudden to say, "That tug that I hired to you for $50.00 an hour is all of a sudden $500.00 an hour, because you're all of a sudden in a pickle." And so your position was that you had an obligation to your valued customers.

Admiral Moran: That's correct.

Captain Searle: The anomalous thing, however, is that in the modern era the big Dutch towing companies and salvage companies are one, but they only came together after World War II, not before World War II. Before World War II they were separate, and that Foundation Company in Halifax wasn't a towing company; it was a salvage company. So the position that the Moran organization has always taken, as I understand it, is that they are really in the towing and transportation business, not rescue.

John T. Mason, Jr.: You mentioned the combination of services as a European concept, did you?

Captain Searle: That's right, and I don't know how they get away with it.

Admiral Moran: They do it, and they've got strong support from Lloyds.[*]

Captain Searle: Yes.

---

[*] Lloyds of London is one of the world's best-known insurance underwriters.

Admiral Moran: Lloyds favor them in many ways—preferential insurance rates on the vessels that are towed by these European people, as opposed to others. But we just feel that our system is a good system, it helps our customers, helps our friends, and makes new friends on many occasions.

Captain Searle: Yes, it does.

John T. Mason, Jr.: And you certainly have evidence to prove that it's a good system.

Admiral Moran: Yes, and what's a most important facet of our policy is that we just tow the ship. If the ship is on the beach or in otherwise serious trouble which we cannot deal with, we make no attempt to handle the problem.

John T. Mason, Jr.: When one of your tugs arrives on the scene and discovers what the situation is, then it is up to the discretion of the tugboat?

Admiral Moran: The tug has been instructed to go and get the ship. If the tug master finds, upon his arrival there, that he cannot accomplish the task that he's been assigned for reasons that are extraordinary or beyond the tug's capability, then, of course, he would make no misrepresentation as to what he is about to do.

Captain Searle: The important thing is that the Moran approach represented themselves as a towing-service company, not a salvage-service company. The towing-service company goes and renders a towing service, and, in fact, the tug is not the commander of the ship. The commander of the ship gives orders to the tug man. But when a salvor takes a tow, the salvor gives orders to the captain of the ship. There's a very subtle and very distinct difference, but that's the core of the problem with the *Amoco Cadiz* case on the coast of Brittany this past March.* That's the real crux of the problem. But Moran has always taken the position that they're not salvors. I'm not sure it's a position I've

---

* The tanker *Amoco Cadiz* ran aground off the coast of Brittany, France, on 16 March 1978, spilling 68.7 million gallons of oil. It currently is number six on the list of the largest oil spills of all time.

always agreed with, but it's certainly a position that's been consistent and has been a valuable one to know.

John T. Mason, Jr.: Is that a similar policy to that espoused by Crowley on the West Coast, up in Seattle?

Admiral Moran: I don't think so, but I'm not certain about what Crowley does with his own tugs.

Captain Searle: Would any of the other tug companies on the East Coast—McAllister, Dalzel, and so forth, Curtis Bay before you bought them—were they ever interested, or did they ever have a flirtation with the salvage business, or did they always have the same kind of a policy as you had?

Admiral Moran: They never had equipment capable of doing what we do, even in the earliest stage. We went out in 1920, and we picked up a ship of the International Marine called the *Minnesota*. Captain Roger Williams was the marine superintendent for the United States Lines at the time. He reached me on the telephone one night and told me that that ship was disabled and asked if we could help. We had a tug that was coming from the east into Long Island Sound. We were able to intercept the tug at New London and send it to the ship, and the vessel was brought into New York. That tug was 150 feet long and capable of about 1,000 horsepower. This was a real big ship, but she towed her in. We got the job. That was the first rescue job that we ever had charge of, and Captain Williams was delighted with the result of it.

Captain Searle: And you charged him on a straight towing basis?

Admiral Moran: We charged him on a straight towing basis.

John T. Mason, Jr.: Admiral, you underscore the fact that this policy of yours was possible largely because you were a big outfit.

Admiral Moran: And we had a tug somewhere near.

John T. Mason, Jr.: In contrast to some of the other companies along the East Coast that were not able to do it.

Admiral Moran: Yes.

Captain Searle: The interesting thing about this policy is that it would appear that the international shipping interests are coming back to that kind of a policy again. Not so much that kind of a policy of charging, but that kind of a policy as to who's in charge.

You see, when a huge tanker or any kind of a vessel that's capable of terribly polluting the coast of some country is in distress off that country, the potential to the strand is horrendous. Public interest doesn't allow the salvage company and the owner to be handy. It has to be understood right away that the tugboat that goes to perform the service will, in fact, perform a service in behalf of the owners of the vessel. The owners of the vessel must call the shots. And so there are many people, including myself, and I noticed a front-page editorial in *Lloyd's List* just this last month or two where someone in France has taken the position that the day of Lloyds's open forum "no cure, no pay" is past, that the public interest doesn't support that kind of position.* It wasn't public interest; it was good business that was pushing your policy.

Admiral Moran: That's right.

Captain Searle: You can't screw anybody, whether he's a present customer or a potential customer, and the business of Lloyds's open forum and that kind of a salvage award is taking too much advantage of a person in distress. It's just inimical to good business. That's what's going on in the public interest. I think your policy was way ahead of its time.

---

* In the traditional no cure, no pay practice in the salvage business, a potential salvor could decline to take on a given job if he deemed the risk to be too great.

Admiral Moran: Well, we took it a long time ago, and we're still doing it. We just sent a tug halfway to Europe to pick up an American-flag tanker and tow her to Portugal, and we did it on a lump sum, rather than daily rates.

John T. Mason, Jr.: And this is a larger scope today. You can send it halfway to Europe.

Admiral Moran: Yes, it's the same principle. We don't own any part of the ship we saved. The salvor feels that he's entitled to a part of a vessel. After he's got the thing finished he wants it in cash.

John T. Mason, Jr.: It's sort of related to booty, isn't it?

Captain Searle: Well, it is like booty. But there's another side of the coin, and that other side of the coin will get us into the World War II situation and perhaps in the present in the English Channel and perhaps off the East Coast of the United States, and that's this.

As the economic pinch on a company gets tighter and tighter, a company can no longer afford to have a plenitude of tugs. It can't afford to have extra tugs, as you used to have, so the present management of Moran and other companies try to be super-efficient and maximize the use of their equipment. When the equipment isn't being used, it's so expensive. They have to pay off the crew and lay up the ship. Now, there is no suitable standby capability, as there wasn't in World War II when all of the tugs began to be used for the transportation of things and the submarines began to sink things on the East Coast. Of course, we had radio. People would call in and say, "Hey, I've been torpedoed," or, "I've lost a propeller, and send somebody to help me."

Now, in the present time, when huge cargoes of oil or hazardous cargoes of anhydrous ammonia are going in and out of Tampa, Florida, or liquid natural gas in and out of Savannah or the Chesapeake Bay, what happens if one of those ships is in distress off the coast, and Moran, McAllister, and everybody else has no commitment to keep a fire engine in the firehouse or a tug at the entrance to the harbor? Where is the capability to protect the public interest?

Let's go to the World War II situation. As I understand it, the naval salvage service was strictly involved in stranding, sinking, and so forth. The Navy and the naval salvage service took over Merritt-Chapman, and Scott. A lot of them went to the European theater and the Pacific theater. But then there was established a Navy rescue-towing service, particularly on the East Coast that I know about, where each naval district had several tugs. The first tugs they had were what were called the ATOs. These were often steam tugs. They were a nondescript lot, and some of them dated to World War I. They were the fire engines in the firehouse that were sent out.

Did Moran participate in that service?

Admiral Moran: The rescue service during World War II was sponsored by the War Shipping Administration. The War Shipping Administration authorized and requisitioned for use a number of coastwise tugs that had the capability of going to sea and towing disabled vessels afloat. There were nine tugs used in the service.

Captain Searle: Nine of your tugs?

Admiral Moran: No, nine commercial tugs.

Captain Searle: But were they all Moran's?

Admiral Moran: No.

John T. Mason, Jr.: That were appropriated by the government?

Admiral Moran: Yes. They were requisitioned for use under Section IX of the 1936 Merchant Marine Act. These tugs were stationed in New York, in Norfolk, and in Miami. They did miscellaneous towing for the War Shipping Administration, vessels that required repair or renewals at a point where they were not at the time of the need, and the Maritime Commission tugs or the War Shipping Administration tugs were used to tow these vessels around, but one tug was assigned to join convoys organized in the gulf, proceeding out of the gulf, up the East Coast to destinations north of Hatteras.

These tugs were something over 150 feet long and 1,000 shaft horsepower, steam propelled. They did a number of striking rescues, the most important one of which was a vessel called the *Wakefield*, which took fire 300 or 400 miles north and east of Halifax. The ship was returning to the United States with injured soldiers and returning civilians who were taken aboard the cruiser *Brooklyn*. Four tugs were sent to the ship and towed her to Halifax safely. A destroyer escort maintained antisubmarine watch for the trip, and the vessel remained in Halifax until she was ready to continue her voyage to Boston, where two of the rescue tugs went back to Halifax and brought the ship down. That was the most notable rescue because the vessel was in constant danger from enemy action while there in disabled condition. The tugs, of course . . .

John T. Mason, Jr.: They were vulnerable, too, weren't they?

Admiral Moran: . . . were vulnerable, because the progress with a ship afire was not rapid. I suspect that they were able to tow her at about five knots. The reason four tugs were sent was because it was thought that in the event of the disability of one or two of the tugs, two at least could get the ship in.

That was one of the most important jobs. It is also interesting to note that out of this fleet of rescue tugs only one was lost as a result of enemy action, and it was the tug *John L. Williams*, which struck a mine off Cape Henlopen.

Captain Searle: Whose tug was that?

Admiral Moran: It was owned by the Great Lakes Dredge and Dock Company.

Captain Searle: Is that right?

John T. Mason, Jr.: But under the aegis of the War Shipping Administration.

Admiral Moran: Yes, the captain and the engineer and two seamen were lost on this occasion. It was the only lost American tug that I can recall in that rescue service.

Captain Searle: Who commanded the rescue service? Did the Eastern Sea Frontier commander?

Admiral Moran: Yes.

Captain Searle: Were there just those nine tugs, or were any of the Moran tugs taken into that service?

Admiral Moran: Yes, there were some in there.

Captain Searle: What about your people? I'm tickled to death that you weren't pressed into the mundane rescue-towing service in behalf of the Eastern Sea Frontier, but rather you were sent to Normandy, to Eisenhower's staff. But were any of your people from Moran taken into the rescue-towing service?

Admiral Moran: Yes. When I left, Captain Earl Palmer took over the job.

John T. Mason, Jr.: Well, Admiral, wasn't it true also that the Navy commissioned the building of some tugs, intending to operate them and then deciding instead to turn them over for operation by skilled tug people?

Admiral Moran: That was the Maritime Commission. Looking at the scarcity of shipbuilding facilities, they were persuaded by the cement industry to build concrete barges, and the commission decided to go forward with the project and let contracts on the East Coast and Gulf, I think, for the construction of a number of concrete barges which, it was felt, would replace the needed ships for overseas transportation or those that were put out of action by an enemy.

The concrete barges would be of no use if there were no tugs to tow them. So the Maritime Commission decided, on completion of the concrete barge program, to build 50 seagoing tugs of about 200 feet in length and 2,250 horsepower.

John T. Mason, Jr.: Monsters for that day.

Admiral Moran: There's no doubt about that.

Captain Searle: These were called ATs?

Admiral Moran: No, these were V-4s.

Captain Searle: V-4 tugs, oh, yes.

Admiral Moran: The concrete barge program never really was accomplished, and the Maritime Commission had 50 tugs surplus to any of their known needs. There was, however, a requirement for tugs by the Navy, and the Navy, knowing of the existence of 50 tugs, felt that they ought to be taken and operated by the Navy. But, on research and investigation, it was found that the manning by the Navy of tugs of this character would require more personnel than the Navy had.

John T. Mason, Jr.: What did one tug of that size require in the way of crew?

Admiral Moran: One tug of that size with a gun crew was manned by 36 men.

Captain Searle: The civilian manning was 36?

Admiral Moran: Yes. The ATF, of about the same capability, except the ATF didn't have the endurance that the Maritime Commission tugs required. The Navy tug was manned by upwards of 100, so the Navy decided to assign its towing requirements to the Maritime Commission and the War Shipping Administration, which had assigned the management and operation to a civilian towing company. The performance of the 50 tugs was really a notable accomplishment.

John T. Mason, Jr.: Somewhere along the line I had the statistics.

Admiral Moran: Yes, you do.

John T. Mason, Jr.: A remarkable number of nautical miles were traveled.

Admiral Moran: I don't remember how many dry docks were towed to the Southwest Pacific, but there is an accurate record of that. There is also an accurate record of the number of ships—I think it was 518—towed from various points in the Atlantic and the Pacific as far west as the South Pacific and as far east as the Mediterranean and Africa, back to the United States.

Captain Searle: These were disabled ships, as a rule?

Admiral Moran: Disabled ships as a rule, yes.

Captain Searle: The civilian management of those tugs, was that Moran, or was that several towing companies?

Admiral Moran: It was just one, because there was only one at the time that was capable of supplying the manpower.

John T. Mason, Jr.: There again, size was a requisite.

Admiral Moran: Yes. Merritt-Chapman, and Scott, Captain Davis, was offered the opportunity of manning as many as he could. He would have first choice, if he wished it, because he had the competence to handle that size vessel and undertake the sort of task that they would be confronted with. He wrote a letter to the Maritime Commission and the War Shipping Administration recommending Moran and regretting his inability to furnish the personnel because all he could do was salvage operations.

John T. Mason, Jr.: And you didn't lose any of those tugs, did you?

Admiral Moran: No.

Captain Searle: So Merritt was running the salvage.

Admiral Moran: Yes.

Captain Searle: And you were running the point-to-point tow business, as distinct from rescue towing.

Admiral Moran: Yes.

Captain Searle: Now, the towing of a disabled ship back from Casablanca or someplace is really a ship-delivery type function and not a rescue tow; that's from point to point.
    Let's get back to the rescue-towing service. You were talking about Captain Palmer. I don't remember him.

Admiral Moran: He was a veteran. When I was detached from the Eastern Sea Frontier on temporary duty to Normandy, my assistant was an admiralty attorney called O'Kane. He had administrative competence, but he didn't have operating competence, so Captain Palmer was taken by the Eastern Sea Frontier to operate—

Captain Searle: He was a Moran hand?

Admiral Moran: He was an ex-Moran captain, yes.

Captain Searle: Let's go back to the Eastern Sea Frontier. When you first came into the Navy, you were at the Eastern Sea Frontier. What were you doing there?

Admiral Moran: I was then in charge of the rescue service.

John T. Mason, Jr.: This was under Admiral Denebrink?

Admiral Moran: No, but that's the man I've been trying to think of. He was the captain of the *Brooklyn* that took the crew off the *Wakefield*, and I later had some dealings with Captain Denebrink.[*]

John T. Mason, Jr.: He's the man who wrote that beautiful fitness report for you.

Admiral Moran: Yes, I was telling Bill about that, that he said something complimentary about me.

Captain Searle: When you were running the rescue-towing service, I really want to get some more of that, because that's not documented anyplace. The rescue-towing service is probably the least documented service of the emergency wartime contingency services that I know of. The reason that I'm aware of that is that within the last year the Navy's salvage office called me up and said, "Hey, Bill, there's a requirement in an OpNav instruction that deals with salvage and says that the Navy salvage office will maintain contingency plans for the reestablishment of the Navy rescue-towing service, and we can't find anything about it."

I said, "I don't know anything about it, either, but I have to get my friend, Admiral Moran, to tell me about it."

So, as I understand it, it was put together in the heat of the battle and requisitioned some ships under the 1936 maritime law, and the Eastern Sea Frontier set up a concept of rescue towing distinct from salvage.

---

[*] Captain Francis C. Denebrink, USN, who eventually became a vice admiral.

Admiral Moran: Right.

Captain Searle: The other thing I understand about it is that Admiral Sullivan, whom we all know, was very insistent that the Eastern Sea Frontier not trifle with salvage. The Eastern Sea Frontier wasn't allowed to have anything to do with salvage. The Navy supervised salvage in Washington and in its New York office. In the day when Captain Davis and Captain Scott were still alive, they had their own little private organization that Sullivan ruled with an iron fist.

Admiral Moran: That's right.

Captain Searle: But they gave you guys the rescue-towing service, so to speak.

Admiral Moran: Right.

Captain Searle: Were you the first head of the rescue-towing service?

Admiral Moran: Yes.

Captain Searle: And Palmer relieved you?

Admiral Moran: Yes.

Captain Searle: Palmer kept it during the rest of the war, did he?

Admiral Moran: Yes.

Captain Searle: I presume Palmer has passed away by now?

Admiral Moran: Yes. Captain Davis at times would call on Captain Palmer for towing assistance but nothing relating to salvage. Davis was in charge of that part, and his salvage people were told what to do. If the tug could accomplish it, it did it.

Captain Searle: Yes. The tugs were the nine he requisitioned from private industry, but you also had some old Navy World War I tugs, didn't you?

Admiral Moran: Yes, but they were under the authority of Commander Service Force Atlantic for service.

Captain Searle: They had originally been part of the old ComTrain, commander of the train.*

Admiral Moran: That's right. They were stationed up in Portland, I think, or up in Maine somewhere, some of them. We got some in Normandy.

Captain Searle: What you're implying, I think, is that the Navy kept the old ATOs for their use, and the Navy rescue service was the requisitioned tugs?

Admiral Moran: Yes, that's right.

Captain Searle: Okay, where did the ATAs come in?

Admiral Moran: The ATAs didn't really come in until about 1943. The ATAs were designed for the Navy by a naval architect named Cook, who was employed by a firm whose name I can't remember.

John T. Mason, Jr.: In New York?

---

* In the years before World War II the auxiliary ships that supported the combatants were known collectively as the fleet train.

Admiral Moran: In New York, but the whole power plant of the ATA was proposed by General Motors, George W. Codrington, who employed Cook to design the tugs.

Captain Searle: Now, you're talking about ATA, not ATFs?

Admiral Moran: ATA. He designed these tugs for the British who were using them and obtaining them under Lend-Lease. The tugs were designed and built for the British. Then they proved adaptable for U.S. naval purposes, and a series of them was built for the U.S. Navy.

John T. Mason, Jr.: Where were they turned out, Admiral?

Admiral Moran: They were mostly built in Beaumont, Texas, and there were some built in Boston, a small shipyard there, and there were some built on the lakes.

Captain Searle: Were some of those identified with the rescue-towing service? Were they to augment the rescue-towing service?

Admiral Moran: No, they were operated under fleet management.

Captain Searle: How did they ever augment the rescue-towing service, then? Or were the nine ships adequate for the war?

Admiral Moran: By the time the ATAs were delivered, the submarine menace off the Atlantic Coast had disappeared.

Captain Searle: That's a good point.

Admiral Moran: But some were sent to Europe to assist in the assembling of the artificial harbors on the British coast.

RADM Edmond J. Moran, Interview #5 (9/21/78) -- Page 133

John T. Mason, Jr.: That's when they came under your command?

Admiral Moran: Yes.

Captain Searle: I think you just struck a very important point. The rescue-towing service sort of lost its need as the submarine threat diminished.

Admiral Moran: Right, and the tugs were returned to their owners.

Captain Searle: And that was probably late '43 and '44 then?

Admiral Moran: Yes, that's about the way it worked.

Captain Searle: As I then pick it up in my own career, there was a residual rescue-towing service right down to the end of the war. I guess Palmer stayed at 90 Church Street...

Admiral Moran: Right.

Captain Searle: ...to the end of the war.* As I understand the rescue-towing service, it was run out of the Eastern Sea Frontier but through the district. The district managed its own tugs?†

Admiral Moran: Yes. Well, each owner manned and operated his tugs.

Captain Searle: But under operational control?

Admiral Moran: We would pass the word through up to Eastern Sea Frontier to the tug owner, who was the operator, and he would be charged with the responsibility of sending

---

* The Eastern Sea Frontier command had its headquarters at 90 Church Street in Manhattan.
† The headquarters of the Third Naval District were also at 90 Church Street.

the tug where we told him to. He was paid by the federal government at a charter rate, including men and fuel.

Captain Searle: Was there a specific contract with each owner?

Admiral Moran: Oh, sure, a charter contract. The Maritime Commission took care of that.

Captain Searle: The opcon of the ship was really under Eastern Sea Frontier, through the district, to the tug owner?[*]

Admiral Moran: Yes, it was a weird thing. It was complicated, when you contemplate it.

Captain Searle: Weren't you in uniform by that time?

Admiral Moran: I was, and I'm going to come back to the start of this thing.

I was a civilian working for the Maritime Commission, getting equipment for Great Britain under Lend-Lease in 1940, after their ports had been bombed out by the blitz, assembling tugs and requisitioning them by virtue of the Maritime Commission's authority under the 1936 act. Getting tugs and sending them to Europe to help the British and, on occasion, requisitioning a tug for the Army for building the bases in Greenland.

Now, let me try the background. I organized this rescue service, requisitioned the tugs. Nobody knew what I was doing. Nobody knew what the rates were. The whole thing turned out like the greatest stunt that ever was devised. Because we were at war, everybody was busy doing their own jobs. Nobody had enough time to look into anything I was handling.

At one stage of the game, Lewis Douglas, a very important American, a congressman from Arizona, went down there as a deputy to Admiral Land, who had plenty to do, building ships. He sent me a memorandum one time telling me that it was all right to do what I was doing with respect to the assignment of these tugs and taking on

---

[*] Opcon—operational control.

the jobs. Everybody had something that they wanted done with tugs, and I would take them and do it, and it was all over. Nobody paid anybody any money. There was no accounting, except for the cost of operating the equipment, and that was strictly accounted for.

At one time D. K. Ludwig had a tanker in a British port which had been disabled for some reason or other, I can't remember why, and they wanted it back in the United States. I had a tug in Europe, so I sent it to the ship. We had to join a convoy to come back across the North Atlantic, because the submarine warfare there was going like mad. We put the ship and the tug in a ten-knot convoy, and we towed that ship all the way back to the United States. Ludwig said, "What's the cost?" I said $2,500 per day, and that was the right price.

John T. Mason, Jr.: Ludwig could afford that.

Admiral Moran: Well, it was his underwriter.

Captain Searle: I was to reassure you, getting into that picture, you didn't want to touch on that subject, but I want to get some more into it.

It reminds me of a very famous quotation by Winston Churchill that the British salvage people like to quote.[*] I certainly can't give you the quotation verbatim, but he was sending an "Atta boy, well done" telegram to the British salvage people. He obviously had somebody on his staff who knew the statistics, and he said that in the past period of time, three months or six months, the salvage service had saved and brought into port for easy return to service some huge tonnage of shipping, which it would have taken the shipbuilding industry two years and very dear steel and machinery to replace. The point, of course, being that it's a heck of a lot cheaper to rescue ships than it is to rebuild them or to build new ones.

Admiral Moran: Of course.

---

[*] Winston S. Churchill was Prime Minister of the United Kingdom from 1940 to 1945.

Captain Searle: So now you started this rescue service yourself. You really were the seminal action in the rescue-tow service. However, the rescue-tow service migrated to the Eastern Sea Frontier. How did that happen? Was there some political razzle-dazzle that the Navy wanted to run it, or what?

Admiral Moran: That's where I was. Adolphus Andrews was Commander ESF then.

Captain Searle: Oh, I thought you were working for the Maritime Commission in those days.

Admiral Moran: I was part time assigned to temporary additional duty with the Navy, first with the ESF, so I was spending maybe the beginning of the week at 90 Church Street in New York.

Captain Searle: You were still a civilian then?

Admiral Moran: No, I was a naval officer then. The Navy asked Captain Davis of Merritt-Chapman, and Scott whom to get.

Captain Searle: I see.

Admiral Moran: And Davis said, "Get this guy." I was a civilian then in the Maritime Commission.

Captain Searle: Oh, before you were in the Navy you were a civilian in Maritime?

Admiral Moran: Sure.

Captain Searle: What were you doing there?

Admiral Moran: I was doing the requisitioning of equipment. I took over $21 million worth of yachts, small craft. I had the small craft division of the Maritime Commission. That was even before War Shipping was created.

John T. Mason, Jr.: Such elegant yachts as the *Nourmahal*.

Admiral Moran: Yes, the *Sea Cloud*, all types of things, little tiny things.

Captain Searle: And you were sending those to Britain?

Admiral Moran: Well, the Navy required a lot of small craft. They had a lot of junk out there, some of which was not able to go from here to there, and we had to go out and pick them up and get them back.

Captain Searle: To review, as I hear it, then, you had come down to the Maritime Commission from New York, from Moran, and you were doing this function vis-à-vis small craft for the Maritime Commission.

Admiral Moran: Yes.

Captain Searle: Along about this time, the Navy realized that they needed a rescue-tow service, and they asked Davis—Davis was with Sullivan in the salvage service; they obviously had control. Davis then recommended to the Navy that they get you out of the Maritime Commission, and then they put you in uniform?

Admiral Moran: Right.

Captain Searle: And you were put in uniform as a commander or as a captain?

Admiral Moran: Lieutenant commander.

John T. Mason, Jr.: When the admiral went with the Maritime Commission, he told me yesterday, he divested himself of responsibility to Moran.

Admiral Moran: That's right.

Captain Searle: Oh, yes. Then you were a lieutenant commander, but while you were a lieutenant commander you were still doing some work at the Maritime Commission?

Admiral Moran: Admiral Land wouldn't let me go.

John T. Mason, Jr.: Admiral Land wouldn't let him go.

Admiral Moran: Yes. You saw the correspondence.

Admiral Moran: I certainly did, and he was very reluctant.

Captain Searle: I never knew this aspect of it, that it was Davis who fingered you.

Admiral Moran: Yes.

Captain Searle: How long were you in the tow service at the Eastern Sea Frontier?

Admiral Moran: Well, I was until I left in the winter of '43.

Captain Searle: So you were with the Eastern Sea Frontier for a couple of years?

Admiral Moran: Yes, I was there a couple of years.

John T. Mason, Jr.: I can tell you a similar story about the Navy and radar and how this developed. The man who was in charge of it didn't have any—nobody else knew about it.

Admiral Moran: Nobody knew what I was doing.

John T. Mason, Jr.: So you can repeat this throughout the government. This was happening all over.

Captain Searle: That's the history of the rescue-towing service, and I really never knew that before.

Who did you place in the various districts? Did you pull from Moran and the other tugboat companies as the district rescue officer?

Admiral Moran: No. The way we operated was through the port director, if there was a port director, to transmit orders to the tug.

Captain Searle: So you really ran it as a civilian operation?

Admiral Moran: Oh, sure, that's right. We were towing in convoys. We had to pick up these convoys at Miami. They'd come around and follow the coastline up. We picked them up and had one tug right in the middle, and these fellows would go right along. There's a limit to what tugs can do in heavy weather. Then, when they put them on zigzagging, which they would do—

Captain Searle: A tug doesn't zigzag as well.

Admiral Moran: They don't do very well. When we had that Ludwig tanker in tow, the convoy commodore was going out of his mind.

Captain Searle: Let me put two and two together here. That's the rescue tow, but then the return using these V-4 tugs and other tugs to pull them back from Casablanca and the Med—

Admiral Moran: Anywhere.

Captain Searle: Was that run out of your rescue-towing office in the Eastern Sea Frontier too? Or was that run out of the Maritime?

Admiral Moran: That was run out of the Maritime office. We had a tug and barge division in the Maritime, and they would tell the operator of the tug what do to with the tug.

Captain Searle: Okay, now let's talk a little bit about World War II towing by Moran, not by anybody else, but just Moran.
There's a very magnificent little pamphlet that General Motors put out that I had a copy of years ago but can no longer find, the story of a YTB, a small tug. It was manned by Moran, and you picked some up in Cape Town and towed all over.

Admiral Moran: Yes.

Captain Searle: This tug went from Cape Town to the States, to Alaska. What was Moran doing in the way of ocean towing?

Admiral Moran: It was doing not very much, because the Navy had the best tug they had. War Shipping had—

Captain Searle: The one they requisitioned?

Admiral Moran: Yes, that was one they requisitioned, and then they requisitioned others right out of the builders' yards, that Moran had contracted for. When the Alaska thing was on, when they went up to Alaska—

John T. Mason, Jr.: The Aleutians?

Admiral Moran: The Aleutians campaign, the Moran tugs were in that, but they had been requisitioned by Maritime and were being operated by Moran. Moran opened an office in San Francisco to deal with the South Pacific. For heaven's sakes, if you knew how many dry dock sections we towed out to the Pacific.

Captain Searle: But they were with your own tugs?

Admiral Moran: Well, some of the tugs—the 50 tugs were the V-4s. Moran had sold four tugs before we got into the war to the Navy, and they requisitioned for use, I think, two tugs. But those units were all out.

John T. Mason, Jr.: Admiral, what happened to the necessary work in New York Harbor during this time, when your tugs were requisitioned all over the place? There must have been some need.

Admiral Moran: Well, the commercial activity in New York Harbor diminished considerably because everything was for the Navy. All the ships were loaded with cargo for the Navy and were working through the port director. The Navy let a towage contract for harbor towing, which Moran had nothing whatever to do with, as I remember, though I'm not sure about that. Maybe they did.

There was an outfit that was a creation of the Interstate Commerce Commission which dealt with the problem of intrastate transportation, and the Maritime Commission built about 50 small tugs, 85-foot tugs, harbor tugs. They called them DPCs.

Captain Searle: Who operated those?

Admiral Moran: Every operator in ports where a shortage of small tugs existed.

Captain Searle: The Army used to have a lot of them.

Admiral Moran: Yes.

John T. Mason, Jr.: Admiral, how did their operation in the harbor tie in with the obligations of the Coast Guard for port security?

Admiral Moran: That wasn't in it. What they did was to tow refuse from the city of New York to points of disposal, wait for the railroads, and they had to dock and undock the ships. All of the ship activity was under the direction of the port director, not essentially the operation of the tugs, but the direction of the port, and the direction of the port involved in the sailing and the docking of ships as they came in and the convoys, to take them out to Scotland lightship or Ambrose lightship and start them off on their way to their destination.

Captain Searle: You've mentioned, Admiral, a couple of times towing dry docks to the Pacific and so forth. It's always been my feeling that towage during World War II of dry docks and the Mulberries, all the big structures, was really a precursor of all the big engineering towing that goes on in the North Sea in the oil industry today.

Admiral Moran: Oh, yes.

Captain Searle: That was really the first of that business.

Admiral Moran: Sure.

Captain Searle: I wonder that Moran didn't persist in that business after the war.

Admiral Moran: Of course, we did persist in that kind of business.

Captain Searle: You towed the big dry dock to Holy Loch.

Admiral Moran: Yes, we went on that voyage.* We put two tugs in the trip, and the Navy put two of theirs. Maybe the Navy put three of theirs. We had one section, and the Navy may have had three sections. They had a tanker which was to provide fuel for all of the tugs. We didn't need it as much as the Navy did. And we also had one of our smaller tugs.

Captain Searle: As a rescue tug?

Admiral Moran: No, she took two barges over. The striking thing there was that we had on a tug that towed one of the sections 11 men as a crew, and the Navy's had 60 men.

John T. Mason, Jr.: Quite a discrepancy in personnel!

Admiral Moran: That's right.

John T. Mason, Jr.: As you pointed out earlier.

Admiral Moran: And it's understandable, but I don't think today that there's any point at all in arming a tug.

Captain Searle: No.

Admiral Moran: They can't defend themselves. They never could, really, but it was done as a matter of course. I think that the manpower thing in the Navy—

Captain Searle: It's ridiculous. Sixty men on an ATF or ATA and 11 men on a Moran tug, a very good figure. I would note for the record here that Moran produced an excellent movie of that tow. I don't know whether it's still available or not.

---

* When the Polaris ballistic missile submarine program was established, the submarines had to operate close in to the Soviet Union. To facilitate that, the submarines were based in Holy Loch, Scotland. Support facilities included the tender *Proteus* (AS-19), which arrived at Holy Loch on 3 March 1961, and a floating dry dock. The base was used until the early 1990s, when the advent of the long-range Trident ballistic missile made overseas basing unnecessary.

Admiral Moran: Yes. I don't know either. We have some still on it, hanging on the wall.

Captain Searle: It was a good PR movie.

Admiral Moran: But the thing we have been able to do that the Navy ought to know about or somebody ought to know about—during the Korean thing and the war in Vietnam, during the summer we went across the Atlantic, through the Suez, up the Indian Ocean, to the place. Eleven men, a tug 105 feet long. In winter we went across the Pacific.

Captain Searle: The mainstream that I was getting into there was we had a precursor of the big ocean-towing business, as opposed to harbor tugging, and as opposed to point-to-point liner services.

Admiral Moran: Sure.

Captain Searle: The Moran company continued to do that on an ad hoc basis, and the admiral eventually commissioned to be designed and built the *Alice Moran*, which was one of the biggest tugs in the world at that time. But the company sort of abandoned the big ocean-towing field to the Dutch. Why was that? The Dutch were just less expensive?

Admiral Moran: We couldn't compete. The Dutch wage costs are so low.

Captain Searle: I see.

Admiral Moran: We towed two gold-mining dredges or tin-mining dredges from Tampa down to Sumatra, I think it was, in the Dutch East Indies, with two of the War Shipping tugs before the Dutch could get going again. But when the Dutch got moving, they—

Captain Searle: The Dutch lost all their tugs in the war. After the war was over, we gave the Dutch companies or sold them some ATAs, and both Smit and Weissmuller, the two big Dutch companies, had a fleet of ATAs, which they operated for maybe 10 or 12 years until they got back on their feet, and they subsequently sold them. Two of those Dutch ATAs are still being operated by the French Navy on the French Navy's missile range in the Pacific. I just found that out a few weeks ago. But we really subsidized the Dutch towing people coming back into business, and pretty soon, because of our maritime labor situation, they take over the ocean-towing business.

Admiral Moran: Yes.

John T. Mason, Jr.: But it's more equal now, today, isn't it, in terms of what they pay and what we pay?

Captain Searle: Well, getting there. It's clearly the conclusion borne out by documents, which I'm sure others hold, that I hold that there was a hell of a shortage of tugs. There was a tremendous shortage of tugs, witness the 50 V-4s that were being built and others. There were documents put out by the Navy's salvage office to the fleet, telling them how to husband the tugs that they had, how to schedule them better, and so forth, how to use the V-4 tugs in the rear areas and the ATAs and the ATFs as salvage ships and so forth.

Admiral Moran: Yes.

Captain Searle: The footnote I'm trying to make is that, in contingency planning, we really have to protect our towing industry in the ocean arena. In a wartime situation—this is assuming we fight the kind of war we fought before, which is probably a bad assumption—but if we get into any situation like that or like Korea or even a little bit like World War II, you need a hell of a lot of towing, ocean towing, and if you need it domestically, you've got to protect the domestic industry somehow, so that you've got both the tugs and the seamanship technique.

John T. Mason, Jr.: Is this something that the Navy has a tendency to overlook in peacetime, as it does overlook the need for minesweepers and all that sort of thing?

Captain Searle: I think so.

John T. Mason, Jr.: I mean, it's something that they think of only in terms of, well, when war comes—

Admiral Moran: Yes, I would suppose that the Chief of Naval Operations regards this as an inconsequential kind of thing that shouldn't concern him but somebody else.

Captain Searle: We're really talking about the need to maintain a capability, and I've already mentioned that there is an OpNav instruction which talks about maintaining a salvage capability and a rescue-towing capability, but there is no instruction certainly associated with contingency planning, and there's precious little contingency planning, at least in the Navy, for point-to-point towing. I would like to believe that there might be some contingency planning in the Maritime Administration, but I don't know.

Admiral Moran: I doubt it.

Captain Searle: I doubt it too. But you say that you and Moran are still using the 1936 law for loans and one thing and another for the procurement of equipment?

Admiral Moran: Oh, yes, sure. We're building now, and from time to time what we do is we put a mortgage on a vessel, and the government guarantees 87½% of that. If we don't meet the payments, why, they'll take the tug and sell the bloody thing.

Captain Searle: One last thing on towing as segments of the industry, then I'd like to get into the philosophy of the design of tugs. But the last thing on the segments of the towing industry: there's salvage, rescue towing, point-to-point towing as a liner service, and ad hoc towing of big structures—dry docks, Mulberries, and offshore oil rigs.

Admiral Moran: Yes.

Captain Searle: The other part of towing, where the Navy has the capability and certainly the civilians have a lot of capability is harbor tugging. What kind of interface did you have with harbor tugging in Moran in World War II days, in the between-war days, and so forth?

Admiral Moran: I don't think there was a great problem during World War II and later. The inland tug has changed in some ways, but mainly in respect of the increased power output to meet the design of the larger ships, in handling the larger tanker or the larger passenger ship, because the inland business of freighting, the movement of cargo has diminished by reason of the truck, except on the inland waters, the Mississippi, the Missouri, that system, and the Great Lakes. That system still requires tugs, and they've advanced the design and the power of that equipment. But the inland tug has not changed materially in, let's say, 25 years with respect to motor power.

Captain Searle: The point I'm trying to get at here, the business aspect of it, is why in the world the Navy does harbor tugging in New York, Boston, San Francisco, Norfolk, and so forth when, just like the 10:1 ratio on the ocean tugs towing to Holy Loch, you have a similar ratio of, perhaps not 10:1, but maybe 5:1 or 6:1 on harbor tugging. Even beyond that, the ratio, or the comparison of savvy, just plain capability, the tug people—Moran or McAllister tugs in New York Harbor have 20 or 30 or 40 years on tugs, and sailors have two or three years on tractors on a farm and three or four months on a tug. Why does the Navy persist in doing harbor tugging?

Admiral Moran: I think the first reason is that they think the commercial tugs are subject to labor problems.

John T. Mason, Jr.: Yes.

Admiral Moran: The second reason, I think, is that the Navy tugs are always going to be with them, and they're going to build up a system of operating them, even though it's far more expensive, as they must now know, because the cost of building a Navy tug is much higher than the cost of building a commercial tug. They have to have more accommodations and more communications, more of everything than the commercial tugs needs, because the commercial tug doesn't need it, nor does the Navy tug need it, except they don't know that they don't need it.

Basically, it's pretty hard to tell a naval officer how to run his shipyard or his port. He wants to do that himself. He wants the control, he wants to be able to be sure his orders are carried out the way he wants them, and the general rule is that it's hard to compete with us, and I suppose the political side of it too.

John T. Mason, Jr.: But, you know, Admiral, it's so in contrast with current policy of the Navy to contract out to all these think tanks, and there are a great many of them around. With various problems that they have, they give them to civilians to do under contract. This is in contrast with that.

Captain Searle: There's another reason that I would add to the admiral's, but it's really associated with one of the things he pointed out. It represents shore-duty billets, and there's always a shortage of shore-duty billets.

Admiral Moran: Yes.

Captain Searle: It's a shore-duty billet for enlisted men if they would really only put guys who had three or four or five or ten years' service at sea on the little tugs. That would be good, but unfortunately they put tractor drivers on them sometimes too.

Admiral Moran: Yes, that's right.

John T. Mason, Jr.: You talk about expenses being higher, more costly for the Navy to do it; you have something currently in the news that demonstrates this. It doesn't have to do with harbors, but the *Saratoga* and the refitting or rebuilding of the *Saratoga*, the difference between the commercial and the Navy.

Captain Searle: That's right.

I wanted to get sort of a chapter, a reasonably short chapter—I know you're getting tired, and I want to offer you a drink of iced water or something here first—then I want to talk about the ATF design and the *Alice* a little bit and get to some of my checklist here.

The subject I'd like to discuss a little bit, Admiral, a very current one with the Navy, and the Navy has been asking me for advice, has to do with the design parameters of a good ocean rescue tug. The current interest in the Navy is probably heightened but certainly does not stem from the tragic loss of the *Amoco Cadiz* on the coast of Brittany.

You mentioned in our earlier conversations that the first rescue that you remember Moran doing was about 1920-21, when you towed the *Minnesota* in, and you mentioned that that was a steam tug, 150 feet long and 1,000 horsepower.

Admiral Moran: Yes.

Captain Searle: My sketchy knowledge of your involvement in tug design, I'm sure you had some hand in the specifications of that tug, but I know that you had a hand in the specifications for the improvement of the Moran fleet in the years prior to World War II. You had a major hand in the decisions that the Navy made which led to the design of the ATF. You mentioned in earlier conversations about this naval architect Cook and the ATA, and then we come down and, on your watch after World War II, you went back to Moran to modernize the fleet, and you really led the towing industry in the United States in increasing the horsepower of harbor tugs, and you led the industry in the use of bigger-horsepower tugs in ocean towing. You reduced the number of tugs, for instance, that are used to berth the Queens from—what do you use, five or seven tugs now down to three tugs or something?

Admiral Moran: We went from ten to five, yes.

Captain Searle: And then I think that the last tug that you personally specified was the *Alice*, named after your wife. So could we talk about that spectrum, from the start of 1920, the improvement of the Moran tug in the '20s and '30s to better steam tugs and then go on to diesel?

Admiral Moran: Yes. Today, the ideal oceangoing tug, because of the increased size of the predominant ships on drawing boards and some presently operating, has changed so that very much larger tugs are needed. The ideal, I would think, would be in length at least 225 feet and not more than 240 feet. Draft ought to be made fairly adjustable to meet the requirements of the stranded ship. The vessel ought to be able to trim to meet the requirements of salvage. The power ought to be from 12,000 to 15,000 on the shaft. The ideal vessel would be twin screw, but fuel costs are a factor in the twin screw, obviously. You can get more fuel economy out of a single screw. You get less handling qualities out of a single screw, but the power economy and small handling requirements of a single-screw vessel are more desirable.

The single-screw vessel will require more draft, obviously. You have to swing a much bigger wheel to get the desired horsepower than you would out of the twin screw. You get smaller wheels on a twin-screw vessel. Wheel-propeller control is important, and the pitch ought to be subject to control from pilothouse management, rather than the fixed wheel. The desirable wheel is the controllable-pitch wheel.[*]

The point of towing energy ought to be as near the midships section as can be arranged. The towing machine should be able to take in and pay out as much as 250 fathoms of wire as near to 2½ inches in diameter as possible.

The deckhouse structure ought to contain as few openings to the deck as possible. Therefore, the housing quarters for the crew ought to be on another deck, or a deck that is not subject to the wash of the sea. The pilothouse and control area ought to be probably

---

[*] In a controllable-pitch propeller, the screw turns at a constant number of revolutions per minute; changing the pitch of the propeller blades varies vessel speed.

40 to 50 feet back of the stem. The stem should have no rake at all to it, because frequently the ocean tug is called upon to exert its power on a straight stem, and if a sheared stem or an overhanging stem is involved, damage is bound to result at the top of the shear.

The after end of the vessel should be as full as possible so that the vessel has as much buoyancy as possible from its basic design. A single mast is all that is needed for communication purposes and for compliance with international law as regards the masthead light and the associated lights to the masthead.

The after end of the deckhouse ought to be so fitted that the vessel can be steered, the towing machine operated, and the engine telegraphs ought to be there. Proper arrangements ought to be made on both sides of the main deck, or the upper deck, for a launch capable of being put over without injury to itself in any kind of weather, from either side.

John T. Mason, Jr.: That's quite a vessel.

Captain Searle: That's very much like the *Alice*, as a matter of fact.

Admiral Moran: Yes.

Captain Searle: That's a beautiful ship.
You started to say you hoped the ship would be twin screw, and then you didn't develop that further. What are the advantages of twin screw?

Admiral Moran: Handling capability.

Captain Searle: And the disadvantages are few?

Admiral Moran: The likewise opposition is with a big single screw you've got to get 12,000 horsepower, rather than maybe 5,500 on each, but much smaller wheels, and you can run one wheel one way and the other, the other.

Captain Searle: You mentioned the automatic towing machine, pay in and pay out. When did Moran first go to the automatic towing machine? What was the first one?

Admiral Moran: In 1912.

Captain Searle: A steam machine then?

Admiral Moran: Yes.

Captain Searle: And you've pretty consistently held to automatic towing machines on all your big tugs?

Admiral Moran: Yes.

Captain Searle: There were some very interesting tugs for towing operations in the '20s and '30s, when the oil companies were barging oil from the United States to Europe, Standard Oil Company in particular, and the oil company tanker would be fitted with a towing engine, and it would, in turn, tow another tanker barge.

Admiral Moran: Yes.

Captain Searle: What became of that? Was that successful?

Admiral Moran: Well, that was done by the Standard Oil Company of New York as early as 1908. The captain was named Tom Fenlon, and the tugs—one was the *Security*, and one was the name of a product that they used. The barges were 89, 90, 91, 92, 93, 94, 95, and I think they lifted 4,000 tons apiece. They also carried sail on the barges, and they had good luck. These barges were towed by ships at the outset, but tugs proved safer and more economical in the end.

Captain Searle: Yes. The interesting thing to me was that they had automatic towing equipment.

Admiral Moran: Oh, yes. It's very difficult to get the catenary in there without the towing machine, because the towing machine takes up the slack or gives it more, as is required. The barge and the ship or the ship and the tug, whatever it is. When you're towing a good-sized ship, you have the same problem. When the ship is on one sea and we're on another, the catenary deepens. When we're both on the same seas the catenary stretches out, and the slack is tremendous, because we're pulling about 43,000 or 44,000 pounds' strain on this wire. It's just about that size, about 2½ inches, and something has to go.

Captain Searle: I'm having a very difficult time with the Navy these days. The efficiency experts, the guys who are cutting the pennies, ordered me to design a tug, and I can design a tug very similar to what you just specified, except the towing engine. Someone says, "Well, we've got a lot of good seamen; we'll put them on there, and we will eliminate $100,000 by buying a cheap towing reel, towing winch, as opposed to an automatic machine."

The German tug that picked up the *Amoco Cadiz* did not have an automatic machine. The Dutch tugs do not have automatic machines.

John T. Mason, Jr.: Then they're not general, are they?

Captain Searle: Well, these have always been on Moran tugs.

Admiral Moran: We've always had them.

John T. Mason, Jr.: Have others had them too?

Captain Searle: The Navy has always had them up until the present era. What's the argument that the Dutch and the Germans have made?

Admiral Moran: I don't know what their argument is.

Captain Searle: It's my unadulterated opinion that, especially for rescue tugs, where you have all kinds of hazardous conditions, short scope and so forth, that you can't really call a tug a rescue tug unless it does have an automatic towing machine.

Admiral Moran: Yes. I don't think anybody who argues against towing machines knows what the hell he's talking about.

Captain Searle: Boy, I'll quote you!

Let's talk about the dieselization of your own fleet. You went to it in the '30s, didn't you?

Admiral Moran: Thirty-six.

Captain Searle: Who talked you into that? What was the argument?

Admiral Moran: There was no argument at all. George Codrington was the vice president of General Motors, and he came to that position because he was an engineer for an automobile company called Winton, and he was an engineer on Winton's yacht.[*] They put a diesel engine in there, and he ran it. He was an engineer and knew what the heck he was talking about. Well, Winton sold out to General Motors, and they continued to sell the Winton engine, which was a four-cycle engine.

John T. Mason, Jr.: He put them in submarines, too, didn't he?

Admiral Moran: He put them in submarines. He put them everywhere.

---

[*] The Winton Motor Carriage Company of Cleveland was the first American company to sell a motor car. Alexander Winton, owner of the Winton Bicycle Company, incorporated the company in 1897. The Winton Engine Company began making diesels in 1912.

Captain Searle: The beginning of the Cleveland diesel, wasn't it?

Admiral Moran: Right.

Captain Searle: Did Winton come to you and promote the first diesel in the first tugboat?

Admiral Moran: Well, I'll come to that. I bought a 550-horsepower engine for a little tug that was trading between New York and Toronto through the New York State Barge Canal. That was about as much power as we could get because of the weight of the engine. The draft in the canal is 15 feet, tops, and I couldn't put too much power and also additional fuel in that tug. So I bought the Winton engine, and it was great. We made a ton of money on that thing, so I said to Codrington, "I need another one with a little more power."

He said okay, and he sent me a purchase order to sign. I signed it, and I think a month or two after I signed it, there was no engine, nothing coming. He called me up, and he said, "Look, I can't fill the order."

"You can't fill the order? What am I going to do? We've got two hulls ready to go."

Well, we bought two engines for them from American Locomotive Company, which were unsuitable, so Codrington said, "I'll build you a couple of engines." He built us 268s, I think he called them, high-speed engines, 750 RPMs, and that was the start of the 268s.

Captain Searle: That was the one that went in the submarines?

Admiral Moran: Went in the submarines, right.

Captain Searle: Was he already dealing with the Navy?

Admiral Moran: Oh, he was dealing with the Navy. He was trying to sell them machines. I went out to Detroit to go to the launching of the first two tugs that were up at

Green Bay, at De Forest or whatever that shipyard is. I met Mr. Kettering in the corridor of the hotel I was stopping at, the Book-Cadillac I think it was called.

John T. Mason, Jr.: Charles Kettering?

Admiral Moran: Yes, Charles Kettering. He drove me up there, and he was talking about machinery, whether it was going to work:

I said to him, "You know, if it doesn't work, my name is going to be mud. You know that, don't you?"

He said, "Sure, but it's going to work, and your name is going to be gold, because this is all right."

So we put the two tugs out.

Captain Searle: This was when, '36?

Admiral Moran: I think this was '38.

Captain Searle: That late.

Admiral Moran: That late, yes. I'm pretty sure it was then. We launched the tugs, they went off, and we've never bought machinery from anybody since. They've advanced the thing now. We have five 67s, or whatever they call them. I don't even know now.

Captain Searle: Was there any opposition in your company to going with you?

Admiral Moran: None whatever.

Captain Searle: How about the other tugboat companies?

Captain Searle: They laughed at me. They said, "This guy is going to go broke."

John T. Mason, Jr.: How long did they continue laughing?

Admiral Moran: They haven't stopped.

John T. Mason, Jr.: Oh, they haven't?

Captain Searle: Anyway, that tug, then, or that activity on the part of General Motors and Admiral Moran, became the basis of the powering of the Navy's ATFs.

Admiral Moran: Sure.

Captain Searle: How did the Navy contact you? Was General Motors feeding into the Navy, or was the Navy talking to you directly?

Admiral Moran: I talked mostly about hull design, and I think that the Chief of Bureau of Ships—I guess it must have been Robison.[*] There was another fellow there.

Captain Searle: It couldn't have been the guy before Robbie, because Robbie had it into World War II.

Admiral Moran: The chief didn't deal with me on this. There was a commander, and he went to work for Worthington.

John T. Mason, Jr.: Mumma, Al Mumma?

Admiral Moran: Al Mumma, yes. He works for Worthington Pumps.

John T. Mason, Jr.: He's retired now, I think.

Captain Searle: He was director of R&D for Worthington.

---

[*] Rear Admiral Samuel M. Robinson, USN, served as Chief of the Bureau of Ships from 1940 to 1942.

Admiral Moran: Yes, he was the guy. I was doing more on hulls.

Captain Searle: There was a hell of an argument in the Navy as to whether it was going to be diesel or diesel-electric.

Admiral Moran: Yes, that's the reason the ATF and the ATA and the ARS were all diesel-electric.

Admiral Moran: Sure.

Captain Searle: Because if was General Motors's development of diesel-electric propulsion for the submarine—

Admiral Moran: And we were the fall guys.

John T. Mason, Jr.: The submarines, at that point, were using some sort of a German motor, which wasn't very satisfactory but was very tough.

Captain Searle: Spielstik, but they also used Alcoa.

Admiral Moran: The ex-Chief of the Bureau of Ships was up at Alcoa once, because he called me on the phone, but Alcoa didn't have it.

Captain Searle: How did the Navy, even in the hull business, interface with you, or how did they talk to you, getting your input into the design of the ATF? I've had people tell me that you really designed the ATF.

Admiral Moran: Well, you know, they got hold of me, and I'd sit down and chew the rag with them about the deck structure. The machinery was all decided. I didn't make any remarks on the machinery with them at all, I don't think. I can't recall that I did. They built some right by where I was working at the time. They built some at Staten Island, the Staten Island Shipbuilding Company, I think it was called.

Captain Searle: Was your office in Staten Island in those days?

Admiral Moran: No, we had a shop down there, though. We still have a shop there.

I was interested in the whole thing. The appearance of the tug. The Navy had a lot more gear than we had in ours, equipment or prospective equipment.

Captain Searle: And the appearance of the tug is just like you describe it: straight stem, flush deck, automatic towing engine, long fantail, full body.

Admiral Moran: Yes, and we designed a body that looks like that, because in a following sea we get picked up very quickly, because, you know, everything is so bad back there. Men are working under the hawser board, you know, the board that goes over the rail of the tug, the taffrail.

Captain Searle: Yes, it was a very critical design characteristic. You've got to prevent the stern from being pooped.[*]

Admiral Moran: Right, you can't have that.

Captain Searle: What about the automatic towing engine? Did the Navy argue against the automatic towing engine?

Admiral Moran: Not to me.

Captain Searle: They just copied your design?

Admiral Moran: Yes.

---

[*] Being pooped refers to a following sea breaking over the stern of a vessel and landing on deck.

Captain Searle: Had you gone to the Almon Johnson machine by then?

Admiral Moran: I think our early machines were made by either Lidgerwood or a company up in Buffalo called Trout, but they are long since gone.

Captain Searle: Yes, there was a little guy by the name of Smith, I think, with Lidgerwood, who was the engineer of their steam automatic engines.

Admiral Moran: Yes. Well, we had steam.

Captain Searle: Nobody went to the Almon Johnson machine because this was an automatic electric system.

Admiral Moran: I forget. I knew him well. He was in the Whitehall Building for years. We had a great relationship. I respected him. That was all right with me, and he would send me a present now and then, consisting of some admiral, a little statue, miniature statuette, that he got over in England—Nelson or somebody.

Captain Searle: What about the design of tugs subsequent to the World War II tugs? You went into modernizing the fleet. You completely dieselized the fleet after World War II?

Admiral Moran: Sure. I had a lot of problems there, visual problems, seeing out all around the pilothouse. I started on that, putting it in place. Then I got it so that they were seeing everything. There was a reflection all over the place. Well, I had to adjust that, you know, glass all around and the reflections that at nighttime were terrible, lights shining from piers and all that sort of thing. But we simplified that and got it in good shape.

    Now we got pilothouse controls, got them right, got the steering right, got the location of the thing right, and the width of the pilothouse so that when they'd go under the flare of the bow they didn't have problems. And then some of the tugs had very low stacks to get under the flight decks. We gave the Navy all that.

Captain Searle: The people who were designing your tugboats just prior to World War II and certainly during World War II were General Motors subsidiary teams?

Admiral Moran: Yes.

Captain Searle: They did some.

Admiral Moran: Yes, they were really naval architects. Actually, they were more designers of yachts.

Captain Searle: Were they?

Admiral Moran: Yes.

Captain Searle: So you used Tams, then?

Admiral Moran: Tams, right. That's the name of the company. I couldn't think of it.

Captain Searle: Tams was a subsidiary of General Motors?

Admiral Moran: Well, I guess they owned them in the end, yes.

Captain Searle: They did, and then they spun them off. The Hack brothers were—

Admiral Moran: Joe Hack, yes. He was a good designer. He worked for Cook. He designed a lot of our equipment.

Captain Searle: What was your approach to having a house naval architect versus hiring Tams or somebody?

Admiral Moran: I wasn't there when the decision was made.

Captain Searle: I mean back n the late '30s, '40s, and '50s.

Admiral Moran: Well, I thought we couldn't afford to keep an architect on the staff.

Captain Searle: Okay, we're getting to the last chapter now. What about the design of *Alice* and the building of *Alice*? What went into your decision to build *Alice Moran*? And tell us what was the horsepower and size of the *Alice*.

Admiral Moran: The horsepower was 10,000. That was a deal we made with Ludwig. Ludwig had ordered four or five, I forget which, 300,000-tonners, and I went up there and said, "What are you going to do if those bloody ships break down?"
    "I don't know," he said, "we'll get them mended."
    I said, "Who's going to do that for you?"
    He said, "Oh, we'll get somebody."
    I said, "You'd better get in with us and do a tug." So we went in 50-50 on the thing.

Captain Searle: So the *Alice* was really designed and built ostensibly as a rescue tug?

Admiral Moran: Sure, and she cost about $2½ million, maybe a little bit more.

Captain Searle: Built in Japan?

Admiral Moran: Built in Japan, built in Kure. She sat around a little while, and I got it going. One of the things that we did wrong was we had a crew that didn't know what was going on, couldn't do anything. We put an American captain on her, and he couldn't get his message to anybody on the tug. He also couldn't eat the Spanish food! We had a time with them. We were trying to meet European competition in wages, and it was the wrong thing to do. If we had dropped $100,000 in wages, it would have paid ten times over.

The first tow she got ran from Kure to the west coast of England, picked up a dry dock to tow to the Maryland Dry Dock Company, and she got off and started going wrong, and in decent weather the dock broke up. Half of it broke off. The weakness was clear there. The dock couldn't stand anything. And that was the worst thing that could happen on the initial voyage. We had a good price for the job, and we messed it up. One of the German tugs came along and picked up the dock and with the tug, the *Alice*, and brought her into Lisbon, I think. They got fixed up there. The opening was sealed up, and we brought her to Baltimore, and she made it without any trouble. But it was an insurance settlement. I don't know who paid that. Anyway, that was a disaster.

And we picked up a ship in Brooklyn and were towing her to Bremen. This ship broke away from us, and the Germans started to talk, "We'll pick her up, but there'll be no cure, no pay."

So I said to the guy who was running the tug, "Pick up the ship yourself and tow her in. Don't tell me how you did. Do it." Then they picked the ship up and towed her into Bremen all right.

Then we towed a couple of barges from Holland to the west coast of Mexico. Then business died off, and she was in New York and was costing us a lot of money.

Captain Searle: It was unfortunate that she represented then and still represents a major rescue-towing capability on the East Coast of the United States, if we had her.

Admiral Moran: Yes.

John T. Mason, Jr.: You sold her then, did you?

Captain Searle: Sold her to the British, United Towing, and they—

Admiral Moran: They used her for running the contest against the fishermen from Iceland.*

Captain Searle: That's right.

Admiral Moran: She was picking up all the ships. She was out east the last I heard of her.

Captain Searle: I don't know where she is. I've lost track of her.

Admiral Moran: But, you know, the Dutch have got four or five big tugs. They're up, as I understand, in the 20,000-horsepower range.

Captain Searle: It's ridiculous to put 20,000 or 25,000 horsepower on a tug, because you can't put it on the wire; you can't put it on the hawser.

The significance of the *Alice* and the reason I wanted her in this story is that she represented a major rescue-towing capability. And Ludwig, give him credit, had some prescience of what was needed, what was going on, and there is today no big rescue-towing capability. You've got some 6,000, 6,500-horsepower tugs now, but for a 300,000-deadweight-ton tanker, they aren't big enough.

I want to add a little vignette here. We were talking about the dieselization of your fleet and the rest of the tugboat fleet and the importance of your involvement as it related to the Navy, but along about 1966-67 Admiral Moran came in to me. We were having lunch one day. I was the supervisor of salvage at the time.† We got off on the subject of steam tugs and diesel tugs. We were really talking about broken-down tankers.

I don't know if you remember this, but the admiral said to me, "You know, I've got one steam tug left that's in my yard over in Staten Island. We keep it there because now and then in wintertime somebody needs steam to run through the coils of a tanker."

---

* In the mid-1970s Great Britain and Iceland squared off in what were known as "cod wars." Iceland claimed exclusive claim over the fishing rights in a zone that extended more than 200 miles from the nation's coasts. British fisherman sought to operate in the same waters, with the result that both nations sent ships into the area in support of the fishermen's interests.
† Captain Searle was the Navy Supervisor of Salvage from August 1964 to May 1969.

I think somebody in New York had just finished salvaging a tanker for coconut oil. If you can imagine 10,000 tons of congealed coconut oil needing steam, and the admiral said to me, "How in the world can we keep that steam tug in our stock? I have no way to do it." I had absolutely no way to do it, and he didn't either, because the company can't, out of the goodness of its heart, maintain that tug and maintain it in operational condition forever and ever.

This goes back to the same point I'm making about rescue towing. The tug either has to make money, or somebody hast to pay taxes to keep the fire engines in the firehouse. Eventually that tug was scrapped.

Admiral Moran: Yes, she was sold for scrap recently. Well, I think we've worn out the subject.

Captain Searle: I think so. We've got all my notes done.

John T. Mason, Jr.: I want to make one comment. Listening to you this afternoon, and knowing how knowledgeable you are on the subject, if your stepfather could be living today, wouldn't he be happy and proud of you?

Admiral Moran: Yes. In the early part of the thing I was telling Jack about my childhood. My father died when I was five years old, and my mother remarried when I was nine, the captain of a tug, a very nice man, a very cautious sort of fellow, a very particular man who wore a stiff collar, a derby hat, and all the rest of the dignified things of those days. He used to take me with him on the tug. He had a little dog on the tug. He went to a country school in Malden. I don't think he did more than fourth or fifth grade when he went out to work on the Hudson River.

He got in the tug business. At one time he was in the ice business. In wintertime, the Hudson River used to supply all of Manhattan Island with ice. He used to cut the ice, put it in barges, store it for the winter, and in the summer he would bring it down. Then finally he got a job with my grandfather, and he was a singular man, a very respectable man. My stepfather would never consciously tell a lie. He never used bad language.

John T. Mason, Jr.: And he took this little lad and—

Admiral Moran: And he taught me a lot of things, and I taught him a lot of things too. I was around nine at the time, and we used to go out, and he'd let me stay up until 9:00 o'clock, I guess, sometimes. He'd be steering, and in front of him was the binnacle, you know, and there was a shelf under the side of that, and I'd sit up there and watch him. We'd be passing these electric signs in the North River, and he'd say to me, "What does that sign say?"

And I would say, "Transportation," or whatever the word was.

He'd say, "How is it spelled?" And I would tell him how it was spelled.

None of the crew could ever start a meal before he started. When he came down to the mess room, he would sit down and say, "All right," and he would start eating. Nobody would eat before he did. He was a disciplinarian, and he would demand everyone's best, including me. He taught me about cordage sizes and strengths and knots. He taught the compass and charts, steering course, and engine room signals, as well, and rules to prevent collisions, whistle signals, and the lead line.

Captain Searle: Admiral, it's been a super afternoon.

Admiral Moran: I wonder!

John T. Mason, Jr.: It's been great, sir.

Index to the Oral History of
Rear Admiral Edmond J. Moran
U.S. Naval Reserve (Retired)

Alice Moran
   Post-World War II tugboat designed for the Moran Towing Company, 144, 149-151, 162-164

Amoco Cadiz
   Tanker that ran aground in 1978 and spilled oil on the French coast, 119, 149, 153

Army, U.S.
   An Army DUKW amphibious truck was lost while being towed to Monterey Bay, 39-40
   Moran's consulting work on Army craft, 40-41
   Had a major role in the June 1944 Allied invasion of Normandy, 62-63, 66-67, 69, 71, 84

Astor, Vincent
   In World War II leased his yacht *Nourmahal* and later sold it to the government, 51

Bland, Schuyler Otis
   Congressman who complained to the U.S. Maritime Commission during World War II on behalf of constituents, 50

Bradley, Lieutenant General Omar N., USA (USMA, 1915)
   Role in connection with the Allied invasion of Normandy in June 1944, 66-67, 84

Brooklyn, **USS (CL-40)**
   Role in the saving of personnel from the transport *Wakefield* (AP-21) after she caught fire in September 1942, 55, 124, 129

Bull, Captain George S.
   U.S. Salvage Association surveyor who was involved in preparations for the June 1944 invasion of Normandy, 65

Bureau of Ships, Washington, D.C.
   Shortly before World War II Moran gave the Bureau of Ships suggestions concerning the design of Navy tugs, 32-35, 149, 157-159
   Role in the construction of concrete barges in World War II, 58-60

Canada
   In 1918 the Navy refrigerated cargo ship *Ice King* joined a convoy in Canada while en route to Europe, 21-22

The transport *Wakefield* (AP-21) was towed to Halifax after having a fire on board in September 1942, 55, 124

Cherbourg, France
Moran did a survey of the port in mid-1944 to determine its cargo capacity, 106-107

Coast Guard, U.S.
In World War II received a number of craft that had belonged to private citizens, 51-52
During World War II dealt with disciplinary cases that involved merchant marine personnel, 97
Port security work in World War II, 142

Commercial Ships
The paddleboat steamer *General Slocum* burned with great loss of life in 1904, 7
A German U-boat sank the British passenger liner *Lusitania* in May 1915, 11, 13
During World War I the Navy acquired cargo ships for its use, 15-19
In World War II the War Shipping Board contracted for 50 V-4 oceangoing tugs, 49 of which wound up being operated by Moran Towing, 88-98, 126-127, 140-141
Rescue of Liberty ships that lost propellers in the post-World War II period.
The tanker *Amoco Cadiz* ran aground in 1978 and spilled oil on the French coast, 119, 149, 153

Communications
The advent of radio communications in the early part of the 20th century facilitated rescues at sea, 112

Concrete
Planned for use in the construction of cargo barges in World War II, 58-60, 125-126

Convoys
During World War I transatlantic crossings by ships of the Naval Overseas Transportation Service, 21-23
Operation of during World War II, 54-55, 135, 139

Davis, Captain Walter N.
In World War II was vice president of the salvage firm of Merritt-Chapman and Scott, 53-54, 115-116, 127-128, 130-131, 136-137

Douglas, Lewis W.
During World War II served as deputy administrator of the War Shipping Administration, 92-93, 134-135

DUKW
Army amphibious truck that was lost while being towed to Monterey Bay, 39-40

Eastern Sea Frontier
    Command role of Atlantic operations in World War II, 55-56, 125, 128-136, 138-139
    In 1962 directed the towing of the destroyer *Monssen* (DD-798), which ran aground in New Jersey, 36-39

Eisenhower, General Dwight D., USA (USMA, 1915)
    Role in connection with the Allied invasion of Normandy in June 1944, 67, 76, 83-84-85, 99, 104, 108-109

Fire
    The paddleboat steamer *General Slocum* burned with great loss of life in 1904, 7
    Saving of personnel from the transport *Wakefield* (AP-21) after she caught fire in September 1942, 55, 124

Fogarty, Lieutenant Commander Nicholas, USNRF
    Former merchant skipper who commanded the refrigerated cargo ship *Ice King* in World War I, 19, 21-23, 26-27

France
    In 1918 the refrigerated cargo ship *Ice King* delivered food to French ports, 19-20, 23-25, 27-28
    Planning for the June 1944 Allied invasion of Normandy, 62-65, 70, 98-99
    Use of tugboats in connection with the invasion of Normandy, 65-79, 96, 98-105
    Concrete caissons were used to form artificial harbors off the invasion beaches, 70-79, 98-105
    Moran did a survey of the port of Cherbourg in mid-1944 to determine its cargo capacity, 106-107
    The tanker *Amoco Cadiz* ran aground in 1978 and spilled oil on the French coast, 119, 149, 153

General Motors Corporation
    In the 1930s and 1940s produced diesel engines for use in tugboats, 33-34, 154-158, 161

General Slocum
    Paddleboat steamer that burned with great loss of life in 1904, 7

German Navy
    Submarine operations in World War I, 11, 13, 23-24, 111-112
    German submarines laid mines in World War II, 56-57
    E-boat operations in opposition to the Allied invasion of Normandy in June 1944, 75, 96

Great Britain
    Used as a staging base for the June 1944 Allied invasion of Normandy, 66, 68, 70-72, 78-79, 82-87, 98-110

Gunnery—Naval
In 1918 the refrigerated cargo ship *Ice King* fired at a German U-boat in the Atlantic, 23-24
In support of the Allied invasion of Normandy in June 1944, 73

Holy Loch, Scotland
In the early 1960s the Moran Company towed a floating dry dock to the Polaris submarine base at Holy Loch, 142-144

***Ice King*, USS**
Refrigerated cargo ship that was taken over by the Navy in 1918 to deliver food to Europe in World War I, 19-25, 27, 29

John L. Williams
Tugboat that was lost after hitting a mine in World War II, 124-125

Kettering, Charles
Development work over the years for General Motors, 33, 155-156

King, Admiral Ernest J., USN (USNA, 1901)
Role in connection with the Allied invasion of Normandy in June 1944, 67, 76, 84-86, 103-105

Kurtz, Captain Thomas R., USN (USNA, 1901)
In World War II served as chief of staff to Commander Eastern Sea Frontier, 55

Land, Rear Admiral Emory S., USN (Ret.) (USNA, 1902)
Service during World War II as chairman of the U.S. Maritime Commission, 42, 48, 50, 53, 58, 69, 84, 86-87, 89, 93, 99-100, 107, 134

Little, Admiral Sir Charles, RN
British officer who was Commander in Chief Portsmouth during the June 1944 invasion of Normandy, 79-80, 108

***Lusitania*, RMS**
A German U-boat sank this British passenger liner in May 1915, 11, 13

***Manhattan*, SS**
Former name of the Navy transport *Wakefield* (AP-21) that caught fire in September 1942 and was towed to port, 55-56, 124

Maritime Commission, U.S.
Role in the early 1940s in requisitioning private craft for government use, 42-53, 134-138
Connection with salvage operations in World War II, 56

Role in the proposed use of concrete barges in World War II, 58-60
Contracted for car floats to be used in the June 1944 invasion of Normandy, 62-65, 68
Assigned V-4 tugs built in World War II to serve the Navy but with civilian crews, 88-98, 126-127, 140-141

Marshall, General George C., USA
Role in connection with the Allied invasion of Normandy in June 1944, 67, 84-85, 109

Merchant Marine Act of 1936
Application in the early 1940s in requisitioning private craft for government use, 42-44, 47, 123-124, 129, 134-135
Used in later years to facilitate tugboat financing, 146

Merrill, Lieutenant Commander Robert T., USN (USNA, 1910)
During World War I served with the Naval Overseas Transportation Service in New York, 15, 18

Merritt-Chapman and Scott Company
Rescue and salvage operations during various periods, 53-54, 112-113, 115-117, 123, 127-128, 130, 136-137

Mine Warfare
In World War I ships were equipped with otter gears to cut mine cables, 18
German submarines laid mines in World War II, 56-57
The tugboat *John L. Williams* was lost after hitting a mine in World War II, 124-125

Monssen, USS (DD-798)
In 1962, while out of commission, broke away from a tugboat's towline and went aground in New Jersey, 36-39

Moran, Rear Admiral Edmond J., USNR (Ret.)
Parents of, 2, 8, 12-14, 165
Stepfather Thomas Reynolds was a tugboat captain who taught Moran much, 2-5, 8, 11-13, 19, 165-166
Boyhood in New York early in the 20th century, 1-7
Worked 1915-17 as an office boy for Moran Towing in New York, 8-14
In 1917-18 served in the Naval Reserve Force in World War I, 14-28
Work with the Moran Towing Company after World War I, 28-31, 154-156
Service from 1941 to 1943 with the U.S. Maritime Commission, 42-61, 134-138
Role with the Eastern Sea Frontier during World War II in connection with the rescue of damaged ships, 52-54, 128-136, 138-139
Naval service in preparation for and execution of landings at Normandy in June 1944, 62-110

Work with the Moran Towing Company after World War II, 114-119, 142-145, 147-148

Moran Towing Company
Originated in 1860, 1-2
Operations in the early part of the 20th century, 2-13
Changes in the company shortly after the end of World War I, 28-31
Operated tugboats for the government during World War II, 60-61, 88-98, 126-127, 140-141
Concentrated on rescue of disabled vessels rather than salvage, 113-122
Commercial towing business after World War II, 113-122, 142-145, 147-151, 162-163
Work atmosphere among employees in the late 1970s, 110
Phasing out of steam-powered tugboats, 164-165

Mumma, Lieutenant Commander Alfred G., USN (USNA, 1926)
In the early 1940s, while in the Bureau of Ships, was involved in tugboat development, 34, 157-158

Naval Overseas Transportation Service
During World War I operated a fleet of ships that carried troops and cargo to Europe, 15-29

Naval Reserve Force, U.S.
Gathered up and trained men for service in World War I, 14-19

Naval War College, Newport, Rhode Island
During a meeting at the war college in the 1950s Moran was commended for his work in connection with the 1944 invasion of Normandy, 81

Navigation
Coastal navigation by tugboats early in the 20th century, 4-5
On board the Navy refrigerated cargo ship *Ice King* in World War I, 27-29

Netherlands
Work of Dutch towing firms after World War II, 144-145, 153-154, 164

New York City
Ship and tugboat operations in New York Harbor early in the 20th century, 4-7
During World War I the Naval Overseas Transportation Service operated from the port, 15-17
Shipping in the port during World War II, 141-142

Normandy, France
Planning for the June 1944 Allied amphibious invasion, 62-65, 70, 98-99
Use of tugboats in connection with the invasion, 65-79, 96, 98-105

Concrete caissons were used to form artificial harbors off the invasion beaches, 70-79, 98-105

Nourmahal
In World War II Vincent Astor leased this yacht to the government and later sold it, 51

Passaic, USS
Original name for a refrigerated cargo ship that was taken into the Navy in 1918 and renamed *Ice King*, 19-20

Pelham Bay Officers' Training School
Trained Naval Reserve Force officers in World War I, 17-18

Perth Amboy
Commercial tugboat that was shelled by a German submarine in 1918, 111

Planning
For the June 1944 Allied invasion of Normandy, 62-65, 70, 98-99

Polaris Program
In the early 1960s the Moran Company towed a floating dry dock to the Polaris submarine base at Holy Loch, Scotland, 142-144

Propulsion Plants
Engineering casualty on board the Navy refrigerated cargo ship *Ice King* in 1918, 22
Diesel-electric drive for Navy tugs designed shortly before World War II, 32-34, 157-158
Diesel engines in Moran's civilian tugs in the 1930s, 33, 154-156

Queen Mary, RMS
British troopship that Moran rode when going to Scotland in 1944, 82

Radio
The advent of radio communications in the early part of the 20th century facilitated rescues at sea, 112

Ramsay, Admiral Sir Bertram, RN
Served as Allied Naval Commander Expeditionary Force during the June 1944 invasion of Normandy, 71, 99, 108, 110

Rescue at Sea
The advent of radio communications in the early part of the 20th century facilitated rescues at sea, 112
Role the Eastern Sea Frontier during World War II in connection with the rescue of damaged ships, 52-54, 128-136, 138-139

Saving of personnel from the transport *Wakefield* (AP-21) after she caught fire in September 1942, 55, 124

With disabled vessels the Moran Towing Company concentrated on rescue rather than salvage, 113-122

Reynolds, Thomas
Tugboat captain who taught his stepson, Edmond Moran, a great deal, 2-5, 8, 11-13, 165-166

Roosevelt, Eleanor
During World War II heard complaints from people who felt they got insufficient compensation for craft requisitioned by the government, 48-49

Salvage
Role of the commercial firm Merritt-Chapman and Scott over the years, 53-54, 112-113, 115-117, 123, 127-128, 130, 136-137

Navy recovery after the transport *Wakefield* (AP-21) caught fire in 1942, 55-56

Scotland
In the early 1960s the Moran Company towed a floating dry dock to the Polaris submarine base at Holy Loch, 142-144

Ship Design
Shortly before World War II Moran gave the Bureau of Ships suggestions concerning the design of Navy tugs, 32-33, 149, 157-159

In the late 1960s Moran helped the Navy on the design of salvage tugs, 35-36

In recent years the trend has been toward larger, more powerful tugs than in the past, 150-151, 160-162

Stark, Admiral Harold R., USN (USNA, 1903)
Commanded U.S. Naval Forces Europe during the Normandy invasion in June 1944, 62, 64, 69-71, 80, 98, 103, 106-108

Submarine Warfare
German U-boat operations in World War I, 11, 13, 23-24

***Thompson*, USS (DD-627)**
Role in support of the Allied invasion of Normandy in June 1944, 84-85

Training
Moran's stepfather taught him much about tugboat operations in the early years of the 20th century, 2-5, 8, 11-13, 165-166

Naval Reserve officer training at Pelham Bay, New York, in 1917, 17-18

Tugboats
    Operations by the Moran Towing Company in the early part of the 20th century, 2-12
    Coastwise towing on the East Coast in World War I, 111-112
    Shortly before World War II Moran gave the Bureau of Ships suggestions concerning the design of Navy tugs, 32-35, 149, 157-159
    Salvage work on damaged vessels in World War II, 54-56
    Construction of by various shipyards during World War II, 59-60
    Moran Towing Company operated tugboats for the government during World War II, 60-61, 88-98, 126-127, 140-141
    Use of in connection with the June 1944 Allied invasion of Normandy, 65-79, 96, 98-105
    Role in rescue and salvage work, 112-136, 138-139
    In the early 1960s the Moran Company towed a floating dry dock to the Polaris submarine base at Holy Loch, Scotland, 142-144
    In 1962 the inactive destroyer *Monssen* (DD-798) broke away from a tugboat's towline and went aground in New Jersey, 36-39
    In the late 1960s Moran helped the Navy on the design of salvage tugs, 35-36
    Work of Navy harbor tugs, 147-148
    In recent years the trend has been toward larger, more powerful tugs than in the past, 150-151, 160-162
    Value of automatic towing machines, 152-153, 159-160
    Phasing out of steam-powered tugboats, 164-165

United Services Organization (USO)
    In World War II Harold Vanderbilt accepted government compensation for his yacht and donated the money to USO, 50-51

Vanderbilt, Harold S.
    In World War II accepted government compensation for his yacht and donated the money to USO, 50-51

***Wakefield*, USS (AP-21)**
    Transport that caught fire in September 1942 and was towed to port, 55-56, 124

War Shipping Administration, U.S.
    Organized a rescue tug service in World War II, 123-125

War Shipping Board, U.S.
    During World War II contracted for 50 V-4 oceangoing tugs, 49 of which wound up being operated by Moran Towing, 88-98, 126-127, 140-141

Weather
    A heavy storm hit Normandy, France, shortly two weeks after the Allied invasion in June 1944, 67-68, 77, 105-106

World War I
    A German U-boat sank the British passenger liner *Lusitania* in May 1915, 11, 13
    Coastwise commercial towing on the East Coast during the war, 111-112
    Operations of the Naval Overseas Transportation Service, 15-29
    Naval Reserve officer training at Pelham Bay, New York, 17-18
    Postwar demobilization in 1919, 26-27

www.ingramcontent.com/pod-product-compliance
Lightning Source LLC
Chambersburg PA
CBHW080613170426
43209CB00007B/1416